This Book Belongs To

_____

CHALICE YEAR TREASUREBOOK

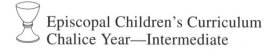
Episcopal Children's Curriculum
Chalice Year—Intermediate

© 1994 by Virginia Theological Seminary and Morehouse Publishing

Text by the editors of Episcopal Children's Curriculum

All rights reserved. No part of this book may be reproduced, stored in a retrieval system, or transmitted in any form or by any means, electronic, mechanical, photocopying, recording, or otherwise, without the written permission of the publisher.

Unless otherwise noted, all Scripture quotations contained herein are from the New Revised Standard Version of the Bible, copyright 1989, by the Division of Christian Education of the National Council of the Churches of Christ in the United States of America and are used by permission.

Developed by
Virginia Theological Seminary
Center for the Ministry of Teaching
3737 Seminary Road
Alexandria, VA 22304

Published by
Morehouse Publishing
P.O. Box 1321
Harrisburg, PA 17105

To Order Additional Copies
Call or Write:

MOREHOUSE PUBLISHING
Harrisburg, PA

Toll Free: 1-800-877-0012

ISBN: 0-8192-6033-9

Sixth Printing, 2002

Chalice Year—Intermediate
Copyright © 1994 Virginia Theological Seminary and Morehouse Publishing

Table of Contents

PART I — Prophets
1. Speaking for God 1
2. Amos 3
3. First Isaiah 5
4. Micah 7
5. Jeremiah 9
6. Ezekiel 12
7. Second Isaiah 15
8. Ten More Prophets (and Daniel) 18
9. The Past and the Future 25

PART II — Jesus and His Parables
1. How Hope Came True 27
2. The Reign of God 30
3. The Messiah of God 33
4. Secret of the Kingdom 34
5. God Is Generous 37
6. More About the Kingdom 39
7. Good Stories 42

PART III — Holy Eucharist
1. Principal Act of Worship 49
2. The Word of God 54
3. Offerings Are Presented 57
4. The Great Thanksgiving 58
5. Receiving and Responding 61
6. Christ Has Died 65
7. Christ Is Risen 67
8. Christ Will Come Again 69

PART IV — Outline of Faith
1. The Catechism 71
2. God in Three Persons 75
3. The Church 76
4. The Creeds 79
5. Sinners Redeemed 81
6. Prayer and Worship 82
7. Christian Ministry 84
8. Christian Hope 86
9. The Spirit Leads 88

PART I.
Prophets

1. Speaking for God

The Bible is called "the word of God." Like no other book, it becomes the voice of God speaking to us. As we listen to the stories and writings from Holy Scripture, the message is clear:
God made us and wants to be close to us.

The long story of God's people begins to unfold in the Hebrew Scriptures, or the Old Testament. From its pages we learn that we were created free to make choices about how we live and how we treat others. But sadly, we make the wrong choices many, many times.

Again and again, we need to hear what God has to say about our situation. No one understood this better than the special servants of God known as "prophets."

Other nations in the Old Testament had kings, but only the Hebrews had prophets. They were not fortunetellers with magic eyes to predict the future. Their role was to "tell forth" their understanding of what God was doing among the nations and in the lives of their leaders.

As teachers, preachers, and writers, the prophets were messengers of God's love and God's judgment. As we read their words in the Bible, we are assured that God never stops reaching out to bring us back to right ways of living.

Moses and the judges who followed him were sometimes called prophets. Two famous prophets of the ninth century BCE were Elijah and his successor, Elisha. Other well-known prophets left writings that now make up a third of the Old Testament. We call them the "literary" prophets. Their work spans about six hundred years.

The Writing Prophets

In the probable order they were written, the list on the next page shows the names and the centuries (BCE) of the Bible's books we call Prophecy.

Amos, 8th   Ezekiel, 6th
Hosea, 8th   Obadiah, 6th
Micah, 8th   Haggai, 6th
Isaiah, 8th (6th)*   Zechariah, 6th (4th)*
Zephaniah, 7th   Malachi, 5th
Nahum, 7th   Joel, 5th
Habakkuk, 7th   Jonah, 5th
Jeremiah, 6th   Daniel, 2nd

*Each of these books is by more than one writer. The Book of Isaiah may have been written by three prophets.

Three longer books are regarded as Major Prophets: Isaiah, Jeremiah, and Ezekiel. Daniel, which is also a long book, is from a much later time.

The other twelve books labeled as prophets are frequently called Minor—but only because of their shorter length.

2. Amos

The Book of Amos is believed to be the first of all the books of the Bible to be preserved in its present form. Certainly Amos was the first of the writing prophets, dating to about 760 BCE.

In his time, the people of God were divided into two kingdoms: Judah in the south, with its capital at Jerusalem, and Israel in the north, with Samaria as its capital.

Amos lived in the town of Tekoa, about six miles south of Bethlehem in Judah. As a shepherd and "dresser of sycamore trees," he took time to be alone and think about what was happening around him. He was sensitive to the presence of God. Probably he went into the cities to sell his wool each year, and there he would watch everything the people were doing. In time, Amos felt called to go north and speak to Israel.

On the surface, everything appeared to be healthy. Many were prosperous, and there was peace. The religious festivals were attended by throngs.

But Amos could see more deeply into the real state of affairs. The people's religion was shallow, and they carried on in wicked living. Luxury and greed were everywhere, while many poor people suffered under their burdens. And Amos recognized that the armies of Assyria, to the east, were in a position to attack and destroy Israel.

In the nine chapters of the Book of Amos, this rural prophet shared parts of at least seven of his sermons. He predicted a grim future for the people of Israel unless they changed their ways. He said that King Jeroboam would die by the sword and the people would have to go into exile.

Amaziah, a priest in the temple at Bethel, told the king what Amos was preaching. Later he warned Amos to leave Israel. "Go back to Judah and prophesy there," Amaziah said. "Don't come back here." (See *Amos 7:10-17*.)

But Amos did not stop his warnings about the judgment of God. He went on to share more visions of a spoiled land, a temple in ruins, and the people of Israel captured and killed. In fact, that is how it all turned out, for in 721 BCE, the Assyrian armies swept over Samaria and took its leaders as captives. They never returned.

The best-known line from Amos' writing is his demand that the people serve their God in sincerity: "But let justice roll down like waters, and righteousness like an everflowing stream." *(Amos 5:24)*.

3. First Isaiah

The Book of Isaiah falls into at least two sections:
A prophet of the eighth century BCE wrote Chapters 1-39. Scholars are not agreed about Chapters 40-66. This portion of the book may be entirely the work of Second Isaiah, in the sixth century. Or it may be that Chapters 55-66 were produced by Third Isaiah, still later.

The first prophet Isaiah was a nobleman who lived in the southern kingdom of Judah. He may have been influenced by Amos. We know only that he prophesied bravely for forty years, following his call from God "in the year that King Uzziah died" (around 740 BCE).

He had gone up to the temple to pray. The light of God's holiness overcame him, and he knew that he and the people to whom he belonged were sinners. After he confessed his own sin, he felt clean and whole again. Then he had a dialogue with the Lord (as described in *Isaiah 6:8-9*):

The Lord: Whom shall I send, and who will go for us?
Isaiah: Here am I! Send me.
The Lord: Go and say to this people . . . .

In the troubled years that followed, Isaiah was faithful to speak words of faith and hope. The mighty army of the Assyrians pressed westward and overwhelmed the Hebrew people. Egypt felt threatened by Assyria and tried to protect itself. Judah, small in territory and numbers of people, was caught between Egypt and Assyria—siding with first one and then the other in an effort to keep the peace and be safe.

Isaiah did not believe that God's people should enter into military agreements with other nations. He taught again and again that God is holy, and that the people should be holy and trust only in God.

Like Amos, Isaiah saw that the people of his land were not living up to God's call for justice. They failed to act uprightly, and their hypocrisy was unmistakable. They deserved to be severely judged. Surely the Assyrian threat was God's way of punishing them for their sins.

In his parable of the Vineyard *(Isaiah 5:1-7),* the prophet declared that God had established a people like a vineyard on a fertile hill. God did everything possible to assure that the vineyard would bring a good harvest. Still, the vines produced only wild grapes! What could God do but let the vineyard go—overgrown and no longer cultivated? God had hoped for justice, but the people produced oppression. God wanted righteousness, but Judah's citizens did wrong and behaved unjustly.

Still, Isaiah had a great vision for the future. He believed that there would always be a faithful group, a "remnant," who kept the law of God. He foresaw a day when a Messiah would come to reign. There would be a new age under the rule of the Prince of Peace, the Anointed One from God.

Following are some of the best-known lines from First Isaiah:

"Come now, let us reason together, says the Lord:
though your sins are like scarlet, they shall be as white as snow;
though they are red like crimson,
they shall become like wool." *(Ch. 1:18, RSV.)*

"Holy, holy, holy is the Lord of hosts;
the whole earth is full of his glory." *(Ch. 6:3b.)*

"The people who walked in darkness
 have seen a great light;
those who lived in a land of deep darkness—
 on them has light shined. . . .
For a child has been born for us,
 a son given to us;
authority rests upon his shoulders;
 and he is named
Wonderful Counselor, Mighty God,
Everlasting Father, Prince of Peace." *(Ch. 9:2, 6.)*

"A shoot shall come out from the stump of Jesse,
and a branch shall grow out of his roots.
The spirit of the Lord shall rest on him,
 the spirit of wisdom and understanding,
 the spirit of counsel and might,
 the spirit of knowledge and the fear of the Lord.
His delight shall be in the fear of the Lord."
 (Ch. 11:1-3.)

"The wilderness and the dry land shall be glad,
 the desert shall rejoice and blossom;
like the crocus it shall blossom abundantly,
 and rejoice with joy and singing." *(Ch. 35:1-2a.)*

4. Micah

Micah was probably a follower of First Isaiah. He was a farmer from Moreshath, a small town about twenty-five miles southwest of Jerusalem.

Samaria, the capital city of Israel in the north, was captured by King Sargon II, of Assyria, in 722 BCE. It seemed that the kingdom of Judah, in the south, would soon be the next to fall before the Assyrian armies.

Isaiah was carrying on his ministry in Jerusalem, and Micah preached in the countryside. Micah was less hopeful, for he believed that even Jerusalem would be destroyed. He said that God loves righteousness even more than the beloved temple. As it turned out, Micah's predictions proved true.

Two passages from Micah's writing are famous. The first is *Micah 5:2:*
"But you, O Bethlehem of Ephrathah,
    who are one of the little clans of Judah,
from you shall come forth for me
    one who is to rule in Israel,
whose origin is from of old,
    from ancient days."

When the Wise Men came to King Herod to ask where Christ should be born, he called the chief priests and scribes to ask them. They replied by sharing the words of Micah. The Messiah was to come from Bethlehem.

The other quotation appears in *ch. 6:8,* at the end of a "lawsuit" in which the Lord is both judge and prosecutor, and the people are the defendants. When the people, in exasperation, demand to know what God wants from them, the answer is given:
"He has told you, O mortal, what is good;
    and what does the Lord require of you
but to do justice, and to love kindness,
    and to walk humbly with your God?"

No one has ever expressed more beautifully what it means to be truly devoted to the will of God. (This passage is quoted in the Catechism of *The Book of Common Prayer,* page 847.)

5. Jeremiah

If you look up "jeremiad" in a dictionary, you discover that it means bitter sorrow or a prediction of doom. This word was coined from the name of Jeremiah, the Hebrew prophet whose ministry covered more than 40 years (approximately 627-585 BCE). Patrick Henry included a jeremiad in a famous speech of 1775 calling for the American Revolution. He said, "Gentlemen may cry, peace, peace—but there is no peace." (See *Jeremiah 8:11*.)

Of all the prophets, Jeremiah is the most fascinating. His life was both sad and heroic. He was constantly involved in strife and suffering, made all the worse by his fearless preaching of a coming doom. He lived under five different kings of Judah and witnessed two sieges of the beloved city of Jerusalem, then two deportations of the people.

Perhaps only a teenager when he was called to be a prophet, Jeremiah was the son of a priest and landowner. The family lived in Anathoth, about an hour's walk northeast of Jerusalem.

We can read about his call in *Jeremiah 1:1-19*. He describes two visions:

• A kettle boiling over. It stood for the threat of the Scythian invaders from the north. They were so cruel that they drank their enemies' blood and wore clothing made by sewing together the scalps of their victims.

• A flowering almond branch. To Jeremiah it meant that he was being chosen by God to tear down what was evil and build up what was right.

During Jeremiah's youth, the Assyrians were the great world power. Then Assyria fell to the Babylonians (or Chaldeans) in 612 BCE. Following that, the Babylonians and the Egyptians struggled for dominance over the whole region. Judah was caught between the two. They became a satellite of Babylonia, but their kings kept trusting Egypt to set them free.

Twice the Babylonian leaders came to Jerusalem with armies to punish her for being disloyal. In the end, the city was destroyed by Nebuchadnezzar.

God's Messenger

All through these troubled times, Jeremiah was the one who spoke for God. His message was never popular, for he had to tell the kings of Judah that they were making mistakes. Both the kings and the people were guilty of grievous sins, Jeremiah declared. He warned that their doom was certain. He told the people to submit to Babylonia, and this caused him to be called a traitor.

Jeremiah pleaded: Trust God. Serve only God. God will restore those who repent and live obedient lives.

We can read of all that was happening during Jeremiah's lifetime in *II Kings, chs. 22-25*. As for the book that bears his name, Jeremiah wrote part of it himself, and some of it he dictated to a scribe (secretary) named Baruch. Possibly the final chapters were written by Baruch alone.

He went through many harrowing experiences. Once he was placed in stocks. *(Jeremiah 20:1-3.)* On another occasion, he was thrown into a muddy cistern, or dungeon, where he might have perished if it had not been for an Ethiopian who came to his rescue. *(Ch. 38:1-13.)*

Jeremiah had a flair for attracting attention to what he needed to say. He visited a potter and saw a clay pot that was defective. The potter re-shaped the clay and made a good pot. Jeremiah said this was a symbol that God could remake the future of God's people in the same way. He warned that they must turn from their ways to avoid disaster. *(Ch. 18:1-11.)*

Later, he bought a clay jug and broke it as a crowd watched. He said that God would break the disobedient nation in the same way, and it would be beyond repair. *(Ch. 19.)*

The Lord showed Jeremiah two baskets of figs outside the temple. In one, the fruit was ripe and tasty. In the other, the figs were too bad to be eaten. The prophet saw the good figs as exiles who would be carried away from Judah, and the bad figs as a disgraced king of Judah and his officials. *(Ch. 24:1-10.)*

Jeremiah put on an ox's yoke and wore it in the streets. He said the nations would all be under the yoke of the king of Babylon, including Judah. *(Chs. 27-28.)*

At one point, Jeremiah asked Baruch to write down a summary of all his prophecies. In the hope of gaining the people's ear, he asked Baruch to take the scroll to the temple and read it aloud. It called on the people of Judah to fear the punishment of God. They must repent of their evil and ask for forgiveness.

Word of this message came to King Jehoiakim, and he was infuriated. He demanded that the scroll be read aloud to him. To show his contempt for what he was hearing, the king would cut off the pages with a knife, as they were read. He threw the pieces into the fire. Then he threatened the life of Jeremiah.

But Jeremiah was kept safe. He wrote his prophecies again, adding more words. This time he predicted that Jehoiakim would die. (See *Jeremiah, ch. 36.*)

A New Covenant

The Book of Jeremiah is not without hope. After the fall of Jerusalem, the prophet wrote *chs. 30-31*. These are sometimes called the Book of Consolation.

In this section he promised that God would restore the fortunes of Israel and Judah. They would be brought back to their land, and their nation would be rebuilt.

He wrote, "The days are surely coming, says the Lord, when I will make a new covenant with the house of Israel and the house of Judah. . . . I will put my law within their hearts; and I will be their God, and they shall be my people. . . . I will forgive their iniquity, and remember their sin no more." *(Ch. 31:31, 33b, 34b.)*

Christians understand that this prophecy has been fulfilled in Jesus Christ. At Holy Eucharist, we hear the words of Jesus spoken on the night of his betrayal: "This is the new covenant in my blood." He was surely referring to Jeremiah's prophecy.

6. Ezekiel

Ezekiel was a different kind of prophet. He went beyond just speaking and writing. He illustrated his teaching in startling ways.

As a young man in his twenties, he left Jerusalem in 597 BCE with the first group of exiles taken to Babylon, and he never returned to Judah. He lived in a house along the canal east of the city, where people would come to hear him teaching.

In the summer of 592, he had a strange vision followed by a call from God to be prophet. His vision is described in *Ezekiel, ch. 1*. He wrote about creatures, faces, wheels, wings, and eyes. Some scholars have compared him to a painter trying to express what can never be understood fully—the holiness, majesty, and ruling power of God.

The book falls into two parts. The first twenty-four chapters were written before the fall of Jerusalem in 587. From Babylon, Ezekiel was looking on as that beloved city moved to its final doom. Just as Jeremiah was being opposed for what he was saying back in Jerusalem, Ezekiel's warnings were very unpopular with his fellow exiles. He continued trying to prepare them for the worst. The people looked ahead to a happy reunion in their land someday. Ezekiel said the reunion would have to be in Babylon!

The second twenty-four chapters were written after the fall of Jerusalem. Now Ezekiel took on a different role. He tried to comfort the exiles who were in despair and sick at heart. He even gave them a code of laws for use when they returned and reestablished their religious observances as faithful Jews. (This code is in the last nine chapters.)

Signs of Coming Doom

We remember Ezekiel especially for the little dramas he performed as "signs" of the doom and punishment that would come to both Israel and Judah:

He built a miniature city and showed it under siege from an iron plate. *(Ch. 4:1-3.)*

He lay down on his left side 350 days (for Israel), then 40 days on his right side (for Judah). All this time he was bound with cords and allowed himself to eat and drink only what he would be allowed during a famine. *(Ch. 4:4-16.)*

He cut off his hair with a sharp sword and divided it into three parts. *(Ch. 5.)*

He dug a hole in the side of his house and carried out the furniture on his back. *(Ch. 12.)*

He ate his bread with quaking and drank his water with trembling. *(Ch. 12:17-20.)*

He did a sword dance to a sharp, ringing song of death. *(Ch. 21:8-17.)*

Words of Hope

In the end, Ezekiel was appreciated for his kind, pastoral care of the exiles. Not wishing to leave them hopeless, the prophet foretold a time when God would give Judah a new heart and a new spirit.

The best example of good news from Ezekiel is his vision of the "valley of dry bones" *(Ezekiel 37:1-14)*.

When he entered the valley, the Lord said him:

"Mortal, these bones are the whole house of Israel. They say, 'Our bones are dried up, and our hope is lost; we are cut off completely.' Therefore prophesy, and say to them, Thus says the Lord God: I am going to open your graves, and bring you up from your graves, O my people; and I will bring you back to the land of Israel. And you shall know that I am the Lord, when I open your graves, and bring you up from your graves, O my people. I will put my spirit within you, and you shall live, and I will place you on your own soil; then you shall know that I, the Lord, have spoken and will act." (See *vs. 11-14*.)

7. Second Isaiah

Beginning with *Isaiah, ch. 40,* we can see that the scene has changed in that book of prophecy. Suddenly we hear no more words of judgment. Instead, here are kindly words spoken to a people who have already suffered enough:

> "Comfort, O comfort my people, says your God.
> Speak tenderly to Jerusalem, and cry to her
> that she has served her term,
> > that her penalty has been paid,
> that she has received from the Lord's hand
> > double for all her sins." *(Vs. 1-2.)*

This is a different writer speaking, with a different kind of message for God's people. Two centuries have passed since the writing of First Isaiah *(chs. 1-39).* It is now about 540 BCE, and there have been some recent developments that were hopeful.

Ten years or so earlier, Cyrus became king of Persia. Within four years he began to march into northern Babylon. The Jewish people saw this as better news, and so did some of the Babylonians as well.

The Persians continued their conquest until, in 539 BCE, the city of Babylon fell. Cyrus was in charge, and the people of God hoped they would be allowed to return to their homeland.

Most Biblical scholars are agreed that Second Isaiah continues through *ch. 55.* The material in *chs. 56-66* is puzzling. It may be more of Second Isaiah, it may be the work of a Third Isaiah, or it may have been produced by several writers.

A New Future

Second Isaiah is very important because he shares a vision of a brighter future for God's faithful people. He wrote about a Suffering Servant who would come to bring salvation.

The early Christians believed that four Servant Songs in Second Isaiah were descriptions of the crucified and risen Jesus Christ, the long-awaited Messiah. He was the One who truly fulfilled the prophet's words. He was the light of the world.

Here are the main themes and lines we remember from the four Songs:

Isaiah 42:1-9. **The Servant will bring justice.**
"Here is my servant, whom I uphold,
my chosen, in whom my soul delights;
I have put my spirit upon him;
    he will bring forth justice to the nations.
He will not cry or lift up his voice,
    or make it heard in the street;
a bruised reed he will not break,
and a dimly burning wick he will not quench;
    he will faithfully bring forth justice." *(Vs. 1-4.)*

Isaiah 49:1-13. **From his birth, the Servant has been prepared to bring light to God's people.**
"And now the Lord says,
    who formed me in the womb to be his servant, . . .
'I will give you as a light to the nations,
    that my salvation may reach to
        the end of the earth.'" *(Vs. 5a, 6b.)*

Isaiah 50:4-9. **The Servant is a humble teacher.**
"The Lord has given me the tongue of a teacher,
that I may know how to sustain the weary with a word.
Morning by morning he wakens—
> wakens my ear to listen as those who are taught."
> > *(V. 4.)*

Isaiah 52:13-53:12. **The Servant is a victim, a man of sorrows.**
"Surely he has borne our infirmities
> and carried our diseases;
yet we accounted him stricken,
> struck down by God, and afflicted.
But he was wounded for our transgressions,
> crushed for our iniquities;
upon him was the punishment that made us whole,
> and by his bruises we are healed.
All we like sheep have gone astray;
> we have turned to our own way,
and the Lord has laid on him
> the iniquity of us all.
He was oppressed, and he was afflicted,
> yet he did not open his mouth;
like a lamb that is led to the slaughter,
> and like a sheep that before its
> > shearers is silent,
> so he did not open his mouth."
> > *(Ch. 53:4-7.)*

Another famous line from Second Isaiah seems to describe that prophet's life and work:

"How beautiful upon the mountains
> are the feet of the messenger
> > who announces peace.

> who brings good news,
> > who announces salvation,
> > who says to Zion, 'Your God reigns.'"
> > > *(Ch. 52:7.)*

8. Ten More Prophets (and Daniel)

Over a period of about three hundred years, ten other prophets put down words that came to them from God. Their names and approximate dates are:

Hosea. Younger than Amos, he wrote about the same time, in the eighth century BCE. He was deeply upset by the idol worship he saw in Israel. He said that the people went after false gods like a wayward spouse who did not remain faithful to her husband. Hosea believed that God was like a loving husband to Israel.

Nahum. He was a patriot from Judah. His book, dating to about 650 BCE, is three poems. The first one speaks of God's power in nature and in human life. He calls on the people to trust this God who can handle their wicked enemies. The second and third songs are pictures of the coming siege, fall, and end of the city of Nineveh. Its two hundred thousand inhabitants and their leaders were destroyed just as Samaria had been.

Zephaniah. Writing around 640 BCE, he began to speak out (as Jeremiah had) about the Scythians—savage invaders who swept southward on their way to Egypt. His theme was "the day of the Lord," a time of final judgment that would include the whole world. Although his short book is mostly doom, he did predict that a righteous remnant of people would survive. (See *Zephaniah 3:1-13*.)

Habakkuk. As a young man in the 7th century BCE, this prophet asked God a penetrating question: Why were the cruel Assyrians allowed to inflict suffering on their neighbors? After some time, he seemed to have an answer: the Babylonians would destroy the Assyrians. But then Habakkuk had to ask God about the wicked Babylonians. He received the answer that "the righteous live by their faith" *(Habakkuk 2:4)*.

No words in Scripture have received greater emphasis than these. The apostle Paul quoted them in *Romans 1:17* and *Galatians 3:11*. So did the writer of *Hebrews 10:38*. Many centuries later they became the battle cry of the Protestant Reformation.

Habakkuk was saying that we can live by faith, no matter what may happen in the world. A full life comes from God's faithfulness to us, and our faithfulness toward God. All are to be faithful to one another, and we should all depend on this. His book ends with a touching psalm:

"Though the fig tree does not blossom,
    and no fruit is on the vines;
though the produce of the olive fails
    and the fields yield no food;
though the flock is cut off from the fold
    and there is no herd in the stalls,
yet I will rejoice in the Lord;
    I will exult in the God of my salvation.
God, the Lord, is my strength;
    he makes my feet like the feet of a deer,
    and makes me tread upon the heights."
(Ch. 3:17-19.)

Obadiah. Written around 575 BCE, this is the shortest prophecy in the Old Testament. But it has an interesting story behind it. Three Biblical families were now enemies of one another: Israelites (descended from Jacob); Edomites (descended from Jacob's twin, Esau); and Nabateans (descended from Ishmael, son of Abraham and Hagar).

Obadiah was a loyal Israelite, and he was upset with the Edomites for not helping when Jerusalem was besieged. Instead, they had helped the Babylonians!

Now, said Obadiah, the Edomites will have to face the Nabateans. He writes to these descendants of Esau:

"Though you soar aloft like the eagle,
    though your nest is set among the stars,
        from there I will bring you down, says the Lord."
(Obadiah 1:4.)

When Obadiah wrote about an eagle's nest, he was probably thinking of a village high in the mountains where the Edomites lived. In time, the Nabateans did bring down the Edomites, just as Obadiah had predicted. They built a great city called Petra where the village had been. But the Nabateans were greedy and cruel. In time, they too were conquered.

Haggai. This prophet's short ministry was devoted mainly to the rebuilding of the ruined temple at Jerusalem. In 539 BCE, Cyrus of Persia allowed Israel's exiles to leave Babylon. A number went at once back to their home land, hoping to restore Jerusalem and its temple. But the task proved too hard, and the rebuilding was delayed. Nearly twenty years went by.

Haggai concluded that the people would never have a better life until they put first things first. They were attending to their own problems and neglecting the Lord's house. He called on them to start building. His book falls into four parts:

1. In the summer of 520 BCE, Haggai sent a message to leaders named Zerubbabel and Joshua, encouraging

them to rebuild the temple. The work began at once, but then it stopped. After a month, Haggai had to urge them on again. *(Ch. 1.)*

2. Haggai predicted that the new temple would be even greater than the earlier one. People of all nations would come to Jerusalem and would acknowledge the rule of God. *(Ch. 1:1-9.)*

3. Haggai delivered a sermon. He acknowledged that the people's fortunes had not improved greatly, but he predicted that God's blessing would soon follow. *(Ch. 2:10-19.)*

4. Finally, Haggai wrote to the governor, telling him that—in spite of all the troubles among nations—God is in control and will finally establish the rule of a chosen servant. *(Ch. 2:20-23.)*

Zechariah. Writing at the same time as Haggai (around 520 BCE), Zechariah's purpose was to assure the returned exiles from Babylon that God would heal and restore the people. He asked the people to put their whole trust in the promises of God. God still cared deeply for the people.

In *Zechariah, chs. 1-8* are eight visions that came to the prophet in dreams, usually interpreted by an angel: The Lord's horsemen patrolling the earth; four smiths shattering four horns; a man about to measure the city; the high priest accused by Satan but defended by the Lord; a seven-branched candlestick supplied with oil by two olive trees; a flying scroll carrying a curse upon thieves and people who swear falsely; a person named Wickedness being removed in a grain basket; four chariots going to and fro in the earth.

The total picture gained from the visions is a restored Jerusalem—prosperous, pure, harmonious. Nations who turn against this city will be destroyed.

The remainder of the Book of Zechariah is two short booklets that are hard to interpret, *chs. 9-11,* and *chs. 12-14.* They were probably written much later by others, perhaps around 300 BCE.

Joel. Written around 500 or later, this prophet's book is a call to repentance, a promise of God's blessing, and a vision of the final judgment of the nations.

Just before he wrote, Joel had witnessed a severe drought and a plague of locusts in Palestine. Locusts travel in swarms, stretching for miles and darkening the sky. They eat grass and leaves, fruit and foliage—everything green and juicy. Then they attack young branches of trees and finally even the hard bark of trunks, leaving the trees white and bare. Inside people's houses, locusts eat linens, woolen garments, and leather items. A famine follows such an invasion of these insects.

Joel believed the locusts were punishment for a people who disobeyed God. He cried out, "rend your heart, and not your clothing. Return to the Lord, your God, for he is gracious and merciful, slow to anger, and abounding in steadfast love, and relents from punishing." *(Joel 2:13.)* The prophet called for a day of national humility and mourning.

Joel stands out as a prophet whose words were fulfilled at Pentecost. Compare *Joel 2:28-29* with *Acts, ch. 2*. He understood that God's purpose would be achieved only if the Holy Spirit were to take possession of humankind.

Jonah. The Book of Jonah was written by an unknown author—no earlier than 500 and possibly as late as 450 BCE. It is not prophecy but a book about a prophet.

The story of Jonah's experiences is well known. He tried to avoid the call of God to go to Nineveh. He was in a storm at sea and thrown overboard. He was swallowed and saved by a great fish that spewed him onto dry land. A bush grew to shade him from the hot sun, and then it was destroyed by a worm.

Jonah had been asked to proclaim destruction to the people of Nineveh, which he did. The people repented of their evil ways, so God had pity on them and did not destroy them. It was hard for Jonah to accept this outcome.

Why is this book in the Bible? Probably because it suggests that God cares about all people, not just the Hebrews. Following their return from the Babylonian exile, the Jewish people had excluded non-Jews and drawn a tight circle around themselves. The writer of Jonah's story made people reconsider God's purpose. After all, the Hebrews were meant to win all people to God, not just their own clan. That was the lesson Jonah learned at Nineveh.

Malachi. This final book of the Bible, written around 500 BCE or later, is the work of a prophet about whom we know almost nothing. He was an observer of God's people and how they lived some years after their return from exile in Babylon. What he saw was very displeasing. God was being cheated by all those who failed to provide proper tithes and offerings. The prophet asked how people could expect good harvests if they failed to recognize God as the source of all things.

People were making offerings of poor quality: rotten bread, blind animals, and lame and sickly creatures. These were not worthy to be given to God. Indeed, no earthly ruler would be satisfied with such things. How, then, could the people expect that God would be?

People were growing weary of worshiping God. Their priests failed to speak God's truth clearly. Marriages were ending casually. People were not keeping their agreements with one another.

The general attitude in this prophet's time seemed to be: What do we get out of trying to be religious and moral? It seems to make no difference one way or another.

So Malachi spoke out. He said the Lord was asking, "Will anyone rob God? Yet you are robbing me!" *(Malachi 3:8a.)*

A Later Book Called Daniel

In our English Bibles, the Book of Daniel appears right after Ezekiel. But it is not like the writings of the prophets. It is "apocalyptic" literature—writing that offers visions of "last things." The New Testament's Book of Revelation is also this kind of writing.

Six of the chapters in Daniel were written in Aramaic rather than Hebrew. Its date is probably about 168 BCE, making it the latest writing in the Old Testament. In Hebrew Bibles, Daniel is part of the third section called Writings.

Nearly everyone enjoys the stories of Daniel. He had great ability to interpret dreams of kings. His friends were thrown into a fiery furnace. God saved them. Daniel was favored by the king. When he would not stop praying to God, he was thrown into a den of lions. God protected him.

It is important to remember the main point of the book: God will rule the universe forever. The day will come when God will bring in a new era of the kingdom of heaven. Nothing can destroy this great plan of God.

9. The Past and the Future

The Hebrew prophets came from many different backgrounds. They saw events from a variety of angles. They shared their messages in many ways. But one main point runs through their writings:

God is the Lord of all history.

The prophets had the courage to speak out for God when kings and religious leaders did not want to hear what they had to say. They called on the people of both Israel and Judah to turn from sin, evil, and selfishness. They urged their listeners and readers to serve God alone, with mercy and justice.

In a very real way, the prophets held up a mirror for us all. How do we look when we peer into it? Do we reflect what God hopes to see in us?

All of us fall short. None of us is free from sin. At times we all love ourselves more than we love others. But Christians share some very good news about our situation. The Messiah, the Suffering Servant, the Son of God—the One of whom the prophets dared to dream—has actually appeared. His name is Jesus of Nazareth.

Jesus' coming was a turning point in human history. All that the prophets hoped for came true in his life, death, and glorious resurrection. Never again would sin and death have the upper hand, for he had defeated these ancient enemies on the cross.

The great saints of the Church are, in a way, the brothers and sisters of the Hebrew prophets. By their example, they too have shown us God's way of righteousness and truth. They tell us to come near to our Lord, resisting firmly any temptation that would prevent us from doing so.

In every generation, we look back to all that God has done. And we look ahead to the promise of the future. The prophets and the saints are our companions, in the great company of God's witnesses. They tell us: God is Lord of all! Rejoice!

PART II
Jesus and His Parables

1. How Hope Came True

Have you ever read something that sounded too good to be true?

That's how it must have seemed each time God's people heard the words of *Isaiah 65:17-25*, written hundreds of years before Jesus was born. A prophet spoke of a time when God would make "new heavens and a new earth."

People would be glad, joyful, and delighted. There would be no more weeping. They would live long, enjoying good harvests and great blessings.

Even before anyone called out to God, every prayer would be heard.

The whole world would be different. The wolf and the lamb would "feed together," and nothing would hurt or destroy others.

For the Jewish people, Isaiah's prophecy was more than just an idle dream. It was a promise that God would restore the beloved city of Jerusalem. God would be with the chosen people and give them hope. They were unsure how such good news could come to pass, but they believed their God would be with them always. They expected great things in their future.

Watching and Waiting

Centuries went by. Nations rose against one another in a troubled world. In the midst of struggle, life for the Jewish people was never like the "new earth" in the prophet's vision. Indeed, the day came when their land was ruled by the government of Rome.

In every generation, the people of God had kept alive the hope that a descendant of the great King David would someday appear as their savior. He would overthrow their oppressors and set them free again. He would reign in Jerusalem, and the world would know that God favored him.

The word for this expected leader was "messiah." It came from the Hebrew and Aramaic languages and meant "anointed one."

Anointing of kings had long been practiced by the Jewish people. The prophet Samuel had prayed to God, the Lord of heaven and earth, as he anointed King Saul with oil. Later, he did the same for David, son of Jesse. These acts of anointing pointed to the future day of the Anointed One of God—the Messiah. (The Greek word for messiah is "Christ.")

The people searched the books of the prophets—Isaiah, Jeremiah, Ezekiel, Micah, and others. Surely these writers who described a new covenant and a new creation must be speaking of an earthly messiah. People longed for a very special kind of king who would be like no other.

God Acted

The day came when God acted to change everything!

Out of Nazareth came a man named Jesus. He attracted many people who wanted to hear him teach. He spoke good news to the poor. He offered forgiveness of sins. He did great works of healing.

But religious leaders did not understand Jesus' message. They became his enemies. In the end, he was sentenced to a cruel death on a cross outside Jerusalem.

Then the impossible happened. Jesus was raised from the dead. His tomb was empty, and he appeared to many people. As the centurion had said on Good Friday, truly this man was God's Son! (See *Mark 15:39*.)

In the weeks and years that followed, Jesus' disciples returned again and again to the story of Jesus' life, death, resurrection, and ascension into heaven. By the power of the Holy Spirit, they came to see that Jesus was God in human flesh. Now the whole world could know in Jesus Christ the very presence of God, Creator of heaven and earth.

Yes, Isaiah and Jeremiah and the other prophets would have understood that God in Christ had changed everything. (Even their own words, written so long ago, meant more than they themselves had understood.) Jesus had died for the sins of all. He had risen from the dead to fulfill the promise of life forevermore. Both sin and death were defeated, and now God had begun "to make all things new."

The hope of God's people had come true.

2. The Reign of God

By the time the Gospels of the New Testament were written, the early Christians were quite sure of what Jesus Christ had done:

He brought the good news of God's kingdom.

Jesus' mission is described in *Mark, ch. 1*. The story opens with an announcement from John the Baptist. John was a messenger preparing the way for the Son of God. He called on people to repent (turn around) and seek forgiveness for their sins. He baptized with water in the river Jordan.

Jesus became a member of the crowd, taking his place along with all those who responded to God's word preached by his cousin, John. He, too, was baptized. At that moment, a voice from heaven said, "You are my Son, the Beloved; with you I am well pleased" *(v. 11)*.

At once, Jesus went into the wilderness. There, for forty days, he was tempted by the Evil One (Satan). But God's angels were with him, and he resisted the temptations.

Upon his return from the desert, Jesus learned that John had been arrested and put into prison. He knew then that his own work must begin. He would make known the "good news" that God's kingdom was now breaking in upon the world.

What Kingdom Is This?

Just what did Jesus mean by "the kingdom of God"? To understand, we must remember that the Hebrew people had come to think of God as *the King*.

As Creator of all that is, God the King ruled in heaven above and in every corner of the earth. All the events in the history of God's people were understood to be mighty acts of the King of the Universe. God had fixed the sun and the moon, the stars, and the whole earth in their places. God cared for humankind and every other creature.

God's people, Israel, knew that no earthly king could ever be the kind of ruler God is. They thought of David and all their other kings of the past as *representatives* of the King of heaven and earth. The power of these kings came from God alone—the One who reigned (ruled) over everything.

Now Jesus was making a very bold claim. He was announcing himself as the Son who shared fully in the kingship of God. He was fully human. But he was not just God's human representative. In him the one and only God was visiting all humankind. What amazing good news from the King of heaven!

In the three short years of Jesus' ministry on earth, he traveled in Galilee, Judea, Samaria, and Perea. He did the work God had sent him to do. Through him the final rule of God was actually planted in the hearts of people.

Jesus' ministry took the form of "teaching, preaching, and healing." That is how the Gospel of Matthew describes his work. (See *Matthew 4:23; 9:35*.)

Jesus proclaimed the reign of God through his parables and also through the miracles he performed. He healed the lame, the blind, the deaf, and the sick. He fed the hungry. But his great deeds were not done merely to impress others, or to make himself popular. His mighty work was done to show that God is stronger than the powers of evil. He wanted everyone to praise God as the One who gave him power.

Now or Later?

Sometimes people have asked: Did Jesus think of the kingdom of God as a part of the *present* time? Or was he pointing to a kingdom of the *future*?

The answer is yes to both questions.

God has always reigned. There is never a time when God is not in charge. So the kingdom is here, now. In Jesus Christ, God has begun to rule in a new way.

Still, we pray for the future kingdom, as Jesus taught us: "Your kingdom come." The full reign of God is still coming into being. It will not be complete until Christ comes again in power and great glory.

We remember these things every year during Advent. The word advent means "coming." In that season we get ready to celebrate the fact that Jesus has already come as a Babe in Bethlehem. But we also look ahead to the day when our risen and ascended Lord will come again.

3. The Messiah of God

Around the time Jesus lived, a number of traveling teachers had attracted followers. Some of these figures were described as messiahs. It was an age of high expectation, for people were thinking and speaking about the coming of someone to lead the people into freedom.

Jesus was different from the very beginning. He called twelve disciples to share in his ministry. Only by leaving everything and following him could these simple "fisher folk" learn what God was doing through the man from Nazareth.

The Twelve heard what Jesus said, and they saw his deeds of power. Now and then they picked up hints that Jesus was the long-awaited Servant of God of whom the prophets had spoken. Finally, after the resurrection and ascension, and following their own Pentecost experience, the disciples knew truly that Jesus was the Messiah of God.

They remembered all that he had taught them. They told and retold his parables.

A New Community

The disciples became "apostles" (persons sent out). They had absolute loyalty to the risen Christ. They spoke his name wherever they went. They taught with new power. The Holy Spirit gave them courage to preach the good news of Christ in their midst. The Church had begun!

Indeed, the Church became a remarkable community of God's Messiah. Wherever people believed in Christ, they shared all that they had. They ate together, prayed for one another, sang hymns, and recalled Jesus' teaching. The world could see that God was shining through their lives.

The story goes on. From Advent to Pentecost, and through all the seasons and weeks in between, the Messiah's people continue to celebrate, year after year. The same good news rings out: God reigns in heaven and on earth.

4. Secret of the Kingdom

Jesus attracted great crowds. On one occasion, we find him sitting in a boat on the Sea of Galilee, with many listeners gathered on the shore. He began to teach in *parables*.

Hebrew teachers had told parables for centuries, but it was Jesus who used them with greatest skill. They were short stories, usually illustrating one main point. A parable caused listeners to use their imaginations and to wonder. Even after a parable was explained, the story might still raise the question: Just what does this mean?

Sometimes Jesus hinted that the meaning of his parables was hidden from the crowds. He intended the parables for his disciples.

Jesus' first parable, found in *Mark 4:3-8,* is usually titled "The Sower." It gives us a picture of a sower scattering seed over an area. Some fell in the path, where birds ate it. Other seed fell on shallow soil full of rocks; it withered soon after coming up. Other seed fell among thorn plants where it was crowded out and could produce nothing. But part of the seed fell on good soil and brought forth grain in great abundance.

When Jesus finished this brief story, he said, "Let anyone with ears to hear listen!" (See *v. 9.*)

Later, when Jesus was with a small group (including the twelve disciples), they asked him about this parable. What had he meant by it?

Jesus answered, "To you has been given the secret of the kingdom of God, but for those outside, everything comes in parables." (See *ch. 4:10-11*.)

What was the "secret" (the mystery) that Jesus had shared with his close followers? Just this: God was doing something new and good in the world. It would meet with opposition, and sometimes evil would seem to overcome the good. But in the end the victory would belong to God.

It was important for the disciples to hold on to this secret and believe it with all their hearts in the months and years ahead. For the crowds of people, it would all be like a riddle until the day when God chose to disclose to everyone the saving good news of the Messiah—so different from anything they had been expecting!

Jesus then explained the parable in detail.

But what if he had not given clues about the story?

What would people have thought the parable was about?

Perhaps they would focus on the *sower*. A sower faces the same conditions every year: Some seed is wasted. Crops depend on seed sprouting and growing in the best possible way. The yield of grain cannot be predicted ahead of time.

But a sower keeps on trying. A sower persists in planting, year after year. A sower trusts that growth and crops will be good enough to make it all worthwhile.

The prophets Jeremiah, Hosea, Zechariah, and both Isaiahs, had spoken of God as a "sower." See especially *Isaiah 55:10-11* for a rich picture of the word of God bringing forth "seed to the sower and bread to the eater."

So Jesus' story can make us think about God as the sower who keeps on scattering seed, generation after generation. The "seed" is God's word.

Then again, perhaps Jesus' listeners thought most about the different kinds of *soil*. Some scholars have thought his story should be called "The Parable of the Soils."

The "path" was hard and had no depth for seed to be covered. The "rocky ground" welcomed the seed but lacked the depth for helping it to grow properly. The "thorns" were so thick they choked out any new plants of a different kind. But "good soil" had the proper qualities for producing a healthy crop.

We can certainly compare the different kinds of soil to the different attitudes of people hearing God's word. And if we do that, we must ask ourselves: What kind of soil are we?

Mark adds an explanation of the parable. It contains more details. The seed is called "the word" eight times!

Early Christians understood that the word is the whole message of the gospel (the whole work of the Messiah in the world).

From Jesus' story, we can understand quite well that we need to accept the good news he brings and allow it to take root in our lives. Only then can we be faithful disciples.

The "Parable of the Sower" is also found in *Matthew 13:3-9* and *Luke 8:5-8*.

5. God Is Generous

"The Parable of the Laborers in the Vineyard" appears only in *Matthew 20:1-16*. It is the story of a landowner who hired laborers for his vineyard at various times in the day.

He went out early in the morning, found some workers, and agreed to pay the daily wage.

His next trip was about nine o'clock. He found workers in the marketplace and hired them. He said he would pay them fairly.

The next two groups of laborers were hired at noon and about three o'clock. Finally, at around five o'clock, the owner hired still others. (This last group said they had been idle all day because no one asked them to work.)

Everyone toiled until evening. It was the custom in Jesus' time for laborers to receive their wages daily at the end of their work period—so the owner called his manager and arranged for everyone to be paid.

They all received the same amount, regardless of when they went to work!

The laborers who were hired first grumbled that the vineyard owner was quite unfair. Since they worked so much longer, should they not have been paid more?

The owner said, "Take what is coming to you, and go on your way. I chose to pay the workers as I wished. Am I not allowed to do what I choose with my own money? Do you envy me for being generous?"

The parable focuses on the generosity of the landowner who gave equal treatment to all.

What Does the Parable Teach?

Jesus was teaching about the reign (kingdom) of God. In this parable, it seems clear that the landowner stands for God who rules over all things. But what are we to make of the laborers and their pay?

Perhaps the story is about God's welcome of non-Jewish people (Gentiles) into the community of Jesus Christ. The first people to receive the good news of the Messiah were Jews. They could think of themselves as the first workers called by the Lord. But in time, it was clear that Christ's message of salvation was for all people.

Should the first hearers of the gospel be favored over the late-comers? The parable says no. In the great generosity of God, everyone stands on equal ground. All are welcome to equal benefits in the Lord's household.

Or maybe the parable is about the Twelve whom Jesus chose. They could have thought of themselves as the first laborers Jesus called. They were the first to enjoy being with him. They gave up their work and their places at home in order to follow the Messiah. But in time there were many others who also became disciples.

Should the earliest followers of Jesus be his all-time favorites? The parable says no. (Indeed, the mother of James and John asked Jesus to grant her sons the places of honor in his "kingdom." This made the other ten disciples angry. Jesus then declared that no one should rule over others among his followers. See *Matthew 20:20-28*.)

The parable teaches: Jew or non-Jew, early or late, we are full participants in Christ's community from the time we respond to his call. God is gracious to share the benefits of the Messiah's reign. No special privileges belong to those who are first admitted to the household of believers. God is equally generous to all.

6. More About the Kingdom

Jesus told many parables about the kingdom (reign) of God—what it is like, and why we should desire it.

Seven of these kingdom parables are found in *Matthew, ch. 13*. The first is the "Parable of the Sower" *(vs. 3-9)*, which is also found in *Mark 4:3-8* and *Luke 8:5-8*. (See Section 4 of this *Treasurebook,* above.)

Of the other six parables, each one begins with the words, "The kingdom of God is like . . . ." Four of these six appear only in Matthew's Gospel:

Weeds in the Field *(vs. 24-30)*. A person sowed a wheat field with good seed. But an enemy planted weeds along with the wheat. Servants asked whether they should try to pull up the weeds. The owner said no. He told the servants they would be pulling up wheat along with the weeds. He asked them to leave the field alone until harvest time. Then the weeds could be gathered and burned, and the wheat could be harvested. (The weeds in Jesus' story were probably darnel—a plant that looks very much like wheat when it is growing.)

What was Jesus teaching with this story? Here is one way of thinking about it:

The field is the world, and all the seeds are the members of the Church. Unfaithful people seem to be present in the Church, along with the obedient and faithful members. God allows this to happen. But a day of "harvest" will come—a time of final judgment when only the righteous members will be saved. For now, we are to be patient and wait.

Hidden Treasure *(v. 44)* and **Pearl of Great Price** *(v. 45-46)*. Someone learned about a field in which a treasure had been hidden. Joyfully, he sold everything he had and bought that field.

In the same way, a merchant found out about a pearl that was very valuable. He sold everything he had and bought that pearl.

These short parables teach the same truth. The reign of God is more valuable than anything else. Jesus was saying to individuals: God's kingdom is worth giving up everything else. Be eager to let God have first place in your life.

Net *(vs. 47-50)*. A large net was thrown into the sea. It caught all kinds of fish. When it was full, the fishers pulled it in, sat down, and sorted the fish. The good ones were kept, but the bad ones were thrown away.

This story is similar to the "Parable of the Weeds" (above). Here is a way to think about it:

God reaches out to bring all kinds of people into the kingdom. No one is excluded. But a future time of judgment will come, when God will separate all who are evil from those who are righteous.

The following two parables from *Matthew, ch. 13,* are found in other Gospels as well. They, too, are about the kingdom of God.

Mustard Seed *(vs. 31-32).* A mustard seed is very small. The mustard plants of Jesus' time grew to a height of ten or twelve feet. It was not really the greatest shrub.

The point of Jesus' story is in the contrast between the size of the seed and the resulting mustard plant. The growth is great and surprising. In the same way, the life of one man, Jesus of Nazareth, seemed to be a small, humble event. But from this single person the reign of God in the whole world was beginning!

See also *Mark 4:30-32* and *Luke 13:18-19.*

Yeast *(v. 33).* When a small amount of yeast is placed with a large amount of flour, the whole bowl of dough swells. Jesus' point is the same as in the parable of the mustard seed: The reign of God grows greatly from a very small beginning.

See also *Luke 13:20-21.*

Jesus' Use of Kingdom Parables

Jesus used his parables of the reign of God for three main purposes:

1. *To warn people that the judgment of God is sure to come.* We cannot be indifferent to the way we practice our religious faith and treat other people. The time is now for taking all such matters very seriously.

2. *To share the good news that the coming kingdom of God will be truly joyful for all people who are now in distress or enduring unfair treatment.* God will take

steps in behalf of the "poor in spirit." People themselves cannot bring about the kingdom through something they say or do. God alone will establish it, for God's nature is love and justice.

3. To make clear what is required as people prepare for entrance into the kingdom. God asks for our devotion. When we do wrong, we are to repent and seek forgiveness from God and other people. We are to act in loving and obedient ways. We are to hold fast to our faith.

7. Good Stories

The Gospels of Mark, Matthew, and Luke include many short parables of Jesus. They follow a pattern of comparing the reign of God to an event or action that would be familiar. Typically, Jesus would introduce these stories with the words, "The kingdom of God is like . . . ."

These three Gospels also contain longer parables of Jesus. They allow us to discover various shades of meaning. They invite us to put ourselves into the scene and feel along with the characters. Or we can imagine how it felt to be one of Jesus' listeners as he told the stories. These longer stories are sometimes called "narrative" parables.

We have already examined one of the narrative parables, **The Sower** (in Section 4 of this *Treasurebook*, above). Like the shorter ones, it is about the kingdom of God.

Here are twelve other narrative parables:

Good Samaritan *(Luke 10:30-37)*. A man was wounded by robbers on the road to Jericho, and left by the roadside. A priest and a Levite passed him by. But a Samaritan took care of him. Who was the neighbor in the story?

Rich Fool *(Luke 12:16-21)*. A wealthy man built larger barns to store his abundant crops. He decided to "relax, eat, drink," and "be merry." God declared him a fool. He stored up treasure for himself but was not "rich toward God."

Rich Man and Lazarus *(Luke 16:19-31)*. A beggar at the gate of a rich man died and was carried away by angels. The rich man also died and went to the place of torment. He begged for relief from the flames. But a great barrier separated the rich man from any such help. He wanted to warn his brothers that they might also die and suffer as he did. But he was told that the brothers should listen to Moses and the prophets.

Unjust Judge *(Luke 18:1-8)*. An unjust judge showed mercy toward a widow. Would not God be even more willing to grant justice to people who cry out for it?

Pharisee and the Tax Collector *(Luke 18:10-14)*. A very religious Pharisee and a tax collector both went to the temple to pray. The Pharisee thanked God that he was not like other people, and that he fasted and gave a tenth of his income to the Lord. The tax collector simply prayed, "God, be merciful to me, a sinner!"

Fig Tree *(Luke 13:6-9)*. A man had a fig tree in his vineyard. It produced no fruit, so he asked a servant to cut it down. The servant asked that it be left for another year and given one more chance to bear fruit.

Great Banquet *(Luke 14:16-24; Matthew 22:1-10)*. A person gave a dinner party, but the invited guests gave excuses at the last minute and did not come. The host sent servants out into the streets to bring in the poor, the crippled, the blind, and the lame. Still there was room for more at the dinner. So people were invited from the roads and lanes. No one who was originally invited would be allowed in.

Unjust Manager *(Luke 16:1-8)*. A manager was wasting the property of the rich man who hired him. Seeing that he was in trouble, this unjust person quickly made shrewd arrangements to collect percentages of money from his master's debtors. The rich man was impressed by the unjust manager's dealings and decided not to dismiss him.

Talents *(Luke 19:12-27; Matthew 25:14-30)*. Servants of an unpopular nobleman were given equal amounts of money to care for while he went away on a trip. When he returned, one had traded and increased his money by a thousand per cent. A second servant had done half as well. But the third servant had simply kept the money hidden away. The nobleman was angry at the servant who made no effort to increase his money, so he took away what he had and gave it to the first servant.

Wicked Tenants *(Mark 12:1-9; Matthew 21:33-41; Luke 20:9-16)*. A man planted a vineyard and went away for a long time. At harvest time, he sent a servant to his tenants and asked for his share of the vineyard's produce. The tenants beat the servant and sent him away. They did the same to two more servants. The owner decided to send his own son. The tenants killed the son, thinking they would get his inheritance.

Two Sons *(Matthew 21:28-32)*. A man had two sons. He asked one to work in his vineyard, but he refused. Then he changed his mind and went. He asked the second son to go to work. This one agreed politely to do so, but he did not go. Which one did his father's will?

Two Debtors *(Luke 7:41-43)*. Two men were in debt to another. One owed five hundred denarii, and the other owed fifty. Neither one could pay. The lender canceled the debt of each one. Which one was the more grateful?

Jesus probably told his stories and waited for people to "get the point" on their own. But in some cases, the Gospel writers have added paragraphs that explain.

When we study a parable of Jesus today, it is a good idea to read just the story itself at first. Think about what it may have meant to the people who heard it. Think also about what it means to you, now. Then read the rest of what Mark, Matthew, and Luke have to say.

Is It a Parable?

Scholars of the New Testament have not agreed on just how many parables the Gospels include. Some lists reach nearly forty in number, others are shorter. It is not always easy to decide whether a short passage is just a simple "saying" of Jesus—or an abbreviated story for which we must fill in the details.

Here are some "undecided" cases: Candle under a bushel basket *(Matthew 5:15-16; Mark 4:21; Luke 11:33);* new cloth on an old garment, and new wine in old wineskins *(Matthew 9:16-17; Mark 2:21-22; Luke 5:36-39).* Are these parables or simply sayings?

What do you think about *Matthew 7:24-27* (also found in *Luke 6:46-49)*? Is this a parable—a story with a meaning that makes us think about God and God's actions? Or is it just some sharp advice on how to respond to all that Jesus has been teaching?

One man was wise and built a house upon a rock foundation. Another man was foolish and built a house upon the sand. When a storm of heavy rain and wind came, the house on a rock continued to stand. The house on sand fell with a mighty crash.

Jesus said that people who listen to his teaching and act upon it are like the wise man. Everyone who hears Jesus but fails to do what he says is like the foolish man.

Some scholars say that the story can only be understood as a strong warning. It does not make us wonder or imagine the way a good parable does.

Other scholars think Jesus meant it as a parable, something like *Jeremiah 17:5-8*—a comparison of a stunted shrub in a parched desert with a tree planted by water. People who turn away from the Lord are like the shrub. People who trust in the Lord are like the well-watered tree.

Also, a very old parable shared by rabbis describes a person who built a house with stone at the bottom and adobe at the top. When heavy rain came, this house stood firm. But another person built a house of adobe with stone at the top. When water came, this house toppled over. The first builder is like a person who does good work while learning Torah (God's teaching). The second builder is like someone who does no good work while learning Torah.

Our Lord Speaks to Us

The Gospel of John, written much later than the other Gospels, contains no parables at all. In this account of Jesus' life, he speaks about himself in poetic language, using "I am . . . " statements:

"I am the good shepherd . . . ."

"I am the door . . . ."

"I am the vine. . . ."

Jesus performs a series of great signs that draw us to him. And he speaks and prays in long passages that move us deeply.

So, no matter which Gospel we turn to, one thing is sure: In our prayerful reading and study, we will meet Jesus. And he will cause us to ask serious questions about our lives. His teaching, like his whole life, turns our minds toward God's reign.

PART III
Holy Eucharist

1. Principal Act of Worship

The Holy Eucharist is like a drama of great power. The service follows long-used patterns, but it is always different. We are drawn into the scenes and teachings of Holy Scripture, and we find ourselves in the presence of

Christ who meets us at the Altar. We are strengthened to "go forth into the world, rejoicing in the power of the Spirit."

All over the world, on Sundays and other days, the Church's people gather to hear the Word of God and to receive the consecrated bread and wine. *The Book of Common Prayer* reminds us that the Eucharist is "the principal act of Christian worship on the Lord's Day and other major Feasts" (p. 13).

The word "Eucharist" comes from *charis,* which is the Greek word for grace. When we "say grace" before a meal we are about to eat, we give thanks for the food God has given us, and we pray for strength to serve our Lord. At our Church's sacred meal of Eucharist, our prayer of grace is called The Great Thanksgiving.

This Christian meal recalls Jesus' Last Supper. He gave thanks for bread and wine and gave them to his disciples with the startling words: "This is my body. This is my blood. Do this in remembrance of me."

Ever since the resurrection, baptized persons have faithfully received Holy Communion at the hands of ministers acting in Christ's name. We offer ourselves to the Lord who receives us at the Holy Table.

Jewish Prayers Were Used

Through the centuries the Eucharist has taken many forms, but the heart of it has never changed. The words of Jesus are repeated, and we remember what he has done for us.

The early disciples of Jesus were Jews. All their lives they had participated in the annual Passover, and they had enjoyed Sabbath meals in their homes. When they gathered at table, they thanked God by saying, "Blessed be God, King of the universe, who brings forth bread from the universe." They broke a loaf of bread and distributed it to everyone.

Following the meal, everyone shared a cup of wine that was blessed by the father in the family. He asked the group to stand and said, "Lift up your hearts." Then he asked permission to give thanks in their name: "Let us give thanks to the Lord our God." The prayer recalled the long history of the Jewish people and pledged continued commitment to God and the community.

Jesus' Last Supper with his disciples surely included these ancient prayers. Later, when they began to celebrate the Lord's Supper, the disciples also used prayers like those of the Sabbath meal.

The Lord's Day

From the beginning, the Church's principal worship has been held on the first day of the week, to recall Jesus' resurrection. It is called the Lord's Day.

Before the end of the period when the New Testament was written, Christians had separated the ritual of the bread and the cup from the regular meals people ate together. It had become too difficult to make room for large numbers who gathered, and the celebration needed to take less time in case the people had to scatter suddenly to avoid persecution.

The early church formed its whole life around the Sunday Eucharist. Before the service, the ministers would move around among the people, greeting them with words of peace and welcome.

The service began simply as the Celebrant said, "The Lord be with you." Then came readings from the Old Testament, Psalm(s), and the New Testament. A stand was provided for the readers. The Celebrant preached from a chair placed where all could see. The "catechumens" (persons not yet baptized) were asked to leave after the sermon.

A deacon then led the prayers, and the Peace was exchanged. A small table was spread with a white cloth. People brought their offerings of bread and wine. The Great Thanksgiving followed (although it had not yet taken a fixed form). After the prayer, the bread was broken and shared by the ministers and people.

More Elaborate Forms

In the fourth century CE, the Emperor Constantine made the Christian faith a legal religion. As the Church was no longer opposed by the government, many more people were welcomed as members. Buildings grew larger, and the services became more elaborate.

"Entrance rites" were developed to help worshipers get ready to hear the Word of God. Many of these rites included a procession of ministers and people. The Gospel book was carried in this procession. Candles and incense were introduced—like those used when government officials appeared at special events. Special prayers of preparation were offered. Hymns and psalms were sung to unite the people as a congregation.

The clergy no longer visited with the congregation before the service. Over the centuries, the entire liturgy grew more formal.

The first English Prayer Book, prepared in 1549 by Archbishop Thomas Cranmer, required that the service begin with a psalm. While this psalm was in progress, the priest said prayers in private.

In 1552, the rites were revised. The psalm was eliminated, and the private prayers were said aloud. The Ten Commandments were included, followed at once by prayers. Various other revisions took place through the years.

How We Begin Today

The Book of Common Prayer used in the Episcopal Church since 1979 includes special forms for beginning the Eucharist at major feasts and other events in the Church's life. Various options are offered throughout the seasons, and these appear in the "rubrics" (directions in italics).

The term "entrance rite" is not used in the Prayer Book, but scholars of liturgy teach us that the following parts of our Service of Holy Eucharist are regarded as a part of this rite (BCP, pp. 323-325 and 355-357):

- *Hymn, psalm, or anthem.* "Hymn" refers to one of the hymns authorized by the General Convention (in *The Hymnal 1982,* or others published by the Church Hymnal Corporation). "Psalms" are from the Prayer Book, pages 585-808. An "anthem" is sung by a choir.
- *The Opening Acclamation.* The first is for normal use, beginning "Blessed be God." The others are used in the seasons of Easter and Lent.
- *The Collect for Purity.* This prayer, for cleansing of hearts, dates to the eleventh century CE. It is required in Rite One but may be omitted in Rite Two.

- *Ten Commandments or Summary of the Law* (Rite One only).
- *The Kyrie/The Trisagion.* "Kyrie eleison" is Greek for "Lord, have mercy." It has been used since the fourth century CE. "Trisagion" is an ancient Greek hymn of the Eastern churches, later introduced in the West. The word means "three holies."
- *Song of praise.* Most often, churches use "Gloria in excelsis" (Latin for "Glory in the highest"). But other suitable hymns of praise may be sung here. Neither the Gloria nor a hymn is used during Advent or Lent.
- *Salutation and Collect.* The ancient salutation, "The Lord be with you," is based on the greeting of Boaz and the response of his reapers. See *Ruth 2:4*.

As early as the fifth century CE, a short prayer, now called a Collect, was included in the entrance rite of the Eucharist. The Collects of the Prayer Book follow in that tradition. (A Collect is a condensed prayer. It has three parts in one sentence.)

2. The Word of God

The first major portion of Holy Eucharist is called The Word of God. After the introductory portion (often called the entrance rite), the ministers and people take part in the following:

- *Readings from Old and New Testaments.* The worship of early Christians focused on the reading of Scriptures, with explanations of their meaning. This pattern was based on the practice in Jewish synagogues.

The readings in the synagogues were chosen by the readers or were a part of an established schedule of readings. Some of the early Christian lectionaries were based on synagogue usage. Very soon, Christian writings were added to the Old Testament (Hebrew) readings. (The word "lectionary" comes from the Latin *lectio,* meaning "a reading.")

Anglicans have always used lectionaries, and these have been revised from time to time. The present lectionary for celebrations of the Eucharist follows a three-year cycle (A, B, C). It is found in *The Book of Common Prayer,* pages 889-931.

The custom of announcing the Scripture lesson dates to the twelfth century CE. Early Anglican Prayer Books required readers to announce the chapter and verse as well as the name of the Biblical book. This may still be done.

The concluding words, "Here endeth the lesson," are from a custom introduced in 1662. The other option is "The Word of the Lord," followed by the response, "Thanks be to God."

The rubrics include the line, "Silence may follow." In many congregations, the readers and people pause for a few moments to reflect prayerfully on the meaning of the Scriptures.

• *Psalm, hymn, or anthem.* From as early as the mid-fourth century CE, Christians have said or sung a psalm after the Old Testament reading. The present Prayer Book permits a psalm after the Epistle as well. Or a hymn or anthem may be used just before the reading of the Gospel.

• *Reading of the Gospel.* The Gospel is always read by a deacon or priest. From the fourth century CE, Christians have stood for this reading. It may be done from a pulpit or from the midst of the congregation. In some churches, the Gospel book is carried to a designated place.

- *The Sermon.* A sermon or homily is required at all celebrations of the Eucharist. This has been true from the time of the first Prayer Book, in 1549.
- *The Nicene Creed.* This Creed, from the Council of Nicaea (325 CE), has been used at the Eucharist since the fifth or sixth centuries, and more widely from the eleventh century on. Anglicans have always included it in the liturgy.
- *Prayers of the People.* From the second century CE, the prayers have followed the readings and the sermon. At times in Christian history, they have taken the form of a litany. The "prayer for the whole state of Christ's Church," in Rite One, has been revised several times since it was written in 1549.

The 1979 Prayer Book places the prayers after the sermon and the Creed. An additional six forms are provided for use in either Rite One or Two *(The Book of Common Prayer,* pages 383-393).

- *Confession of Sin and Absolution.* A confession of sin said by the whole congregation was introduced in the period of the Protestant Reformation in the sixteenth century. Anglican Prayer Books have always included some form of confession.

In Rite One, the first invitation to confess, the general confession, and the words of absolution, were written in 1548. A newer form of the confession is based on a prayer published in England in 1968. The absolution may be followed by one or more sentences of Scripture sometimes known as the "comfortable words."

In Rite Two, the form of the invitation to confess is new to the 1979 Prayer Book.

- *The Peace.* Some students of liturgy trace the exchange of the peace to verses in the New Testament (such as *I Corinthians 16:20, I Thessalonians 5:26,*

Philippians 4:21, and others). The first clear references to this custom are in the early liturgies for Holy Baptism. It faded from use in later Christian history and has been revived only in the twentieth century. Our Prayer Book includes The Peace at the point where it was exchanged in the early Church.

3. Offerings Are Presented

The liturgy of The Word of God is followed by the liturgy of The Holy Communion. It begins with the Offertory that is described in the rubrics of *The Book of Common Prayer,* pages 333 and 361. The Offertory includes:

• *Sentences of Scripture.* From the 1549 Prayer Book on, verses from the Bible have been used to invite people to make their offerings. *The Book of Common Prayer* provides a list of Scripture sentences for this purpose, but still others may be said.

• *Hymn, psalm, or anthem.* During the Offertory, the people or a choir may sing—or there may simply be music provided by an organ or other instrument.

• *Presentation of gifts and preparation of the Altar.* The Prayer Book contains an additional direction, on page 407: "It is the function of a deacon to make ready the Table for the celebration." This practice began as early as the second century CE.

In the early church, sometimes the table was not brought into the place of worship (or moved to the center) until after the prayers of the people. Offerings of bread and wine were brought to the deacons, or the deacons circulated among the people to collect them.

Enough bread and wine for the sacrament was placed on the Altar, and the remainder of the people's offerings was saved for use by the clergy and the poor. Water was added to dilute the wine, and this practice continues today.

In the Middle Ages, the Offertory included a procession and other rituals connected with the presentation of the bread, the wine, and gifts of money for the poor.

In churches where there is no deacon, the celebrant is in charge of preparing the table. The rubrics provide that "representatives of the congregation" are to bring the gifts of bread, wine, and money to the Altar. The people stand for this presentation.

4. The Great Thanksgiving

We call the prayer over the gifts of bread and wine The Great Thanksgiving. It has been offered in many different ways for nearly two thousand years. Some of the prayers have been short, others long.

The Book of Common Prayer contains six forms of The Great Thanksgiving—Eucharistic Prayers I and II of Rite One, and Prayers A, B, C, and D of Rite Two. In all these forms we can observe certain key parts:

• *Opening dialogue.* The celebrant greets the people, using the words, "The Lord be with you," and they respond. Next comes the *Sursum Corda* (Latin for "Lift up your hearts"), and the people's response. Then the celebrant asks permission to give thanks in the name of the congregation. The people respond: "It is meet and right so to do," or "It is right . . . ." This dialogue has been used since the earliest Christian celebrations.

Going Forth

The Great Thanksgiving

Offering the gifts

The Word of God

Gathering

HOLY EUCHARIST

- *Praise and thanksgiving.* The celebrant proceeds with words that thank and praise God. A Proper Preface is included in most forms of The Great Thanksgiving. The forms for this Preface are found in the Prayer Book on pages 344-349 and 377-382. They emphasize specific reasons for offering praise and thanksgiving on particular days and occasions.
- *Sanctus and Benedictus.* The congregation joins the voices of the angels and "the whole company of heaven" in singing the Sanctus ("Holy, holy, holy"). *Sanctus* is Latin for "holy." It may be followed by the *Benedictus* (Latin for "blessed"): "Blessed is he who comes in the name of the Lord."
- *The Words of Institution.* This section proclaims the reason for The Great Thanksgiving. The celebrant tells the story of our sin, of God's mercy, and of Christ's death upon the cross as a sacrifice for us all.

Placing hands upon the bread and the cup of wine, the priest speaks the words of consecration. They include Jesus' own words at the Last Supper: "This is my Body . . . ," and "This is my Blood . . . ."
- *The Memorial Acclamation.* The celebrant and the people proclaim together that Christ has died, is risen, and will come again. This acclamation is the turning point in the prayer.
- *Words of Remembering (Anamnesis).* When we have "amnesia," we do not remember who we are or why we are here. "An-amnesis" is just the opposite. The mighty acts of God in the death and resurrection of Jesus Christ are made very real in our memory. We praise and thank God.
- *The Oblation (Offering).* The priest offers to God the consecrated gifts of bread and wine. In Rite One, the prayer includes an offering of ourselves (our souls

and bodies) as a "reasonable, holy, and living sacrifice."

• *Invoking the Holy Spirit (Epiclesis)*. The prayer continues as the celebrant asks God to send the Holy Spirit upon the gifts and make them holy. Included is a plea that all who take part in the Sacrament may also be blessed by the Spirit. *Epiclesis* is the Greek word for "calling upon."

• *Supplications*. The celebrant now prays that everyone who receives the body and blood of Christ will be faithful in serving God, and that we shall all enter finally into the kingdom of heaven.

• *Doxology*. The Great Thanksgiving ends with a sentence that glorifies Father, Son, and Holy Spirit.

• *The People's Amen*. From the mid-second century CE, the final Amen has been emphasized as a response by all the worshipers at the Eucharist. (Notice that it is printed differently from the other Amens in the Prayer Book.)

• *The Lord's Prayer*. Since the sixth century CE, the Lord's Prayer has followed the people's Amen.

5. Receiving and Responding

Just after the Lord's Prayer, the celebrant at the Holy Eucharist breaks the bread and offers the gifts of bread and wine to the people—just as Jesus shared the loaf and the cup with his disciples at the Last Supper.

Members of the congregation come forward for Communion. Finally, everyone joins in a prayer of thanksgiving, which is followed by the blessing and dismissal.

Each of these acts in the service has a long history:

• *The breaking of the Bread*. The breaking of the bread (called "Fraction") is a symbol of the broken body of Christ on the cross. For many centuries, a single loaf of wheat bread was used, to stand for the unity of our Communion. The breaking was a simple act of sharing; each person received a portion of the one loaf (the one Body).

In time, the Church began to use small, round wafers. The first Prayer Book in 1549 did not end the use of these, but it urged that wafers be larger and thicker so that each one could be broken into at least two pieces. The 1662 Prayer Book returned to the use of a regular loaf of bread. But the nineteenth century brought wafers back into use. Today, both customs are followed.

At the Fraction, the celebrant may say or sing, "Christ our Passover is sacrificed for us," to which the people respond, "Therefore let us keep the feast." These words were in the 1549 Prayer Book but omitted from later versions. Our present liturgy has restored this "anthem." It may be sung by the people, a soloist, or a choir.

The *Agnes Dei* (Latin for "Lamb of God") begins, "O Lamb of God, that takest away the sins of the world." It comes from *John 1:29* and has been used at the Eucharist since the fourth century CE. At times in Anglican history, it has been omitted from the liturgy. In the present Prayer Book, it has been restored as a possible Fraction anthem.

Rite One includes the optional "prayer of humble access," which begins, "We do not presume . . . ." This prayer was included in the first Prayer Book, and it speaks of our humility in receiving so great a gift as the one offered us in the Sacrament.

• *The serving of Communion.* The celebrant offers the gifts to the people with the words, "The gifts of God for the people of God." This is revised from a fourth century Eastern liturgy which read "holy things for holy people." A second sentence, "Take them in remembrance . . . ," dates to the 1552 Prayer Book.

From ancient times, people have stood as they received Holy Communion. This is still the practice in the Eastern and present-day Roman Catholic churches. The practice of kneeling at the altar rail was begun in Anglican churches in the early seventeenth century. The rubrics of *The Book of Common Prayer* say nothing about kneeling or standing.

The words spoken by the ministers as Communion is served have been used since the baptismal services of the early Church. They are based on *Matthew 26:28, Mark 14:24,* and *I Corinthians 11:24.*

Hymns, psalms, or anthems may be sung by the people or by a choir during the Communion.

• *The prayer after Communion.* In the early Church, the Eucharist ended with the people's communion. As congregations and buildings grew larger, a more formal ending was needed to prevent people from scattering without a sense of community.

By the fourth century, a dismissal was added. Soon afterward, a prayer of thanks was introduced. The prayer asks for God's help in living the Christian life. Over time, more prayers and rites were added. But the Protestant Reformation stripped these away. It was important that the people be free to leave the church and carry out their good intentions to serve God and their neighbors.

• *The blessing and dismissal.* In Rite One, the blessing is given by the celebrant, in either of two forms (p. 339). The longer of these forms dates to the first Prayer Book.

No text is provided for the blessing in Rite Two. The celebrant may compose one, or choose from any Prayer Book blessing in today's language.

Four forms are provided for the dismissal. The people respond, "Thanks be to God."

Loving and Serving

One form of the dismissal from Holy Eucharist is "Go in peace to love and serve the Lord." These words remind us that the common prayers of the congregation have ended, but their Christian service is just beginning.

The Eucharist declares powerfully that Jesus made the greatest of all sacrifices because of God's great love for us. Our response (our answer) to this good news must be more than words. We are called to reach out to our neighbors in acts of service.

Our serving begins with those who are closest to us—our families, friends, and neighbors. We can perform acts of kindness. We can show sympathy when others are in trouble, sick, or suffering. We can lend a hand when we are needed.

We, too, are asked to make sacrifices. This means giving some of our time, energy, and money to assist other people. We are called to think of our neighbors' needs as much as we think of our own. It is good to forget ourselves and think about helping others.

The Church offers many opportunities for serving. Other tasks to be done are all around us in the larger community. Christians leave the Holy Table to join in all such good causes. We do so because we prayed to God in this or a similar way:

> Eternal God, heavenly Father,
> you have graciously accepted us as
>   living members
> of your Son our Savior Jesus Christ,
> and you have fed us with spiritual food
> in the Sacrament of his Body and Blood.

Send us now into the world in peace,
and grant us strength and courage
to love and serve you
with gladness and singleness of heart;
through Christ our Lord. Amen.
   (Holy Eucharist, Rite Two, BCP, p. 365)

6. Christ Has Died

In the Gospels, the accounts of the Last Supper make it clear that Jesus was telling his twelve disciples he would die. He predicted that one of them would betray him. When he broke the bread and poured the wine, he spoke of his own broken body and spilled blood.

Jesus' teaching, preaching, and deeds of power had aroused strong reactions from the people who followed him and from the religious authorities (scribes and Pharisees). The crowds wished to proclaim Jesus as the long-awaited Messiah. That was the theme of the spontaneous Palm Sunday procession into Jerusalem. Jesus rode on a donkey as people shouted "Hosanna!" and laid leafy green branches and garments on the road.

The authorities feared the whole idea of Jesus as an earthly ruler. They found every possible way of discrediting his ministry, and they plotted to get rid of him. It was at their direction that Judas was bribed with money to assist soldiers in arresting Jesus.

At the Last Supper, the disciples were greatly puzzled by all that Jesus had said. But they joined in singing a hymn at the end of the meal *(Mark 14:26a)*, and they followed Jesus into the night. At the Mount of Olives, they heard Jesus predict that they would all "fall away"—even Peter.

In the Garden of Gethsemane, Jesus prayed that the will of God would be done, even if it meant that he must die. And then Judas came with a crowd sent by the religious authorities. Jesus was arrested and taken away.

The following day, a hasty trial resulted in the decision of Pontius Pilate to allow Jesus to be crucified, along with two criminals.

The earliest written account of Jesus' passion is found in *Mark 15:16-39*. The story can be divided into three sections:

• *Mocking (vs. 16-20)*. After he was condemned, Jesus had no rights. The soldiers could do with him as they wished. The whole "consort" (battalion) was about 600 soldiers. They stripped Jesus of his clothing, robed him in purple (to suggest he was "king"), and later re-clothed him in his own garments. This whole episode was not a punishment approved by Pilate. The soldiers did it on their own, as a cruel sign of disrespect.

• *Crucifixion (vs. 21-32)*. Death on a cross was the ordinary punishment for slaves who had done wrong. The victim was nailed to a crossbar that was later raised and fastened to an upright post. The feet were nailed or tied to the post.

Simon of Cyrene (in North Africa), probably a black man, was forced by the soldiers to carry Jesus' cross to Golgotha, north of Jerusalem. The name Golgotha means "place of the skull" in the Aramaic language.

Jesus was offered a drink, probably to deaden the pain. Mark reports that Jesus refused it. Because people were crucified naked, the soldiers were free to take their clothing. In Jesus' case, they gambled for his garments.

The men crucified with Jesus may have been involved in an uprising against the Roman government.

• *Death (vs. 33-39)*. Jesus was on the cross six hours—from about nine in the morning until three in the afternoon. This was a short time, since many victims lingered on a cross as long as two days. It was dark during the final three hours of Jesus' agony, from noon onward. Jesus died with a "loud cry," and the curtain of the temple was torn in two, top to bottom.

The centurion who had stood watch the whole time said, "Truly this man was the Son of God!"

Jesus was only thirty-three years old. He had been teaching, preaching, and healing only three years. Now he was lifeless—his body broken, his blood poured out.

7. Christ Is Risen

Jesus' burial place was provided by Joseph of Arimathea, a Jewish leader who may have been a secret disciple. He asked Pilate for permission to take the body, which he wrapped in a linen cloth he had bought. He took the body to his own hewn rock tomb. A large slab of stone was rolled against the entrance.

The day after the crucifixion was the sabbath. It was a time of sorrow and despair for the followers of Jesus. Their teacher lay dead, and their hopes were crushed.

The next morning (on the first day of the week), Mary Magdalene, Mary the mother of James, and Salome went to the tomb to anoint Jesus' body. We can read what happened in *Mark 16:1-8*. They did not see their risen Lord. But a young man dressed in white (an angel), gave them the amazing news that Jesus was not there. He had risen.

Mark reports that the women were so afraid that they "said nothing to anyone" *(v. 8)*.

Years before Mark wrote his Gospel, the apostle Paul had written about appearances of the risen Christ. See *I Corinthians 15:3-8*. The very existence of the Church rested on the glad Easter news, "Christ is risen."

If there had been no resurrection, there would have been no Christians. Nor would we have had the New Testament. For the very heart of our faith rests on the Gospels' accounts of what happened two days after Jesus' death and burial.

'Little Easters'

Sometimes we say that every Sunday is a "little Easter." We can say this because our Eucharist on the Lord's Day is always a celebration of the resurrection of Jesus.

In the liturgy, our Creed includes the sentence, "On the third day he rose again in accordance with the Scriptures."

In Rite One, the Great Thanksgiving recalls Jesus' "mighty resurrection" (pp. 335, 342). And in the prayers of Rite Two also, we rejoice in Jesus' victory over death:

Prayer A: "Christ is risen." "Recalling his death, resurrection, and ascension, we offer you these gifts."

Prayer B: "We proclaim his resurrection."

Prayer C: "We celebrate his . . . resurrection."

Prayer D: "proclaiming his resurrection."

As we move forward to receive the bread and wine of Holy Communion, we are an Easter people who rejoice in the good news that Jesus is our living Lord. He rose again from the dead and sits on the right hand of God the Father.

8. Christ Will Come Again

At our celebrations of Holy Eucharist, each form of The Great Thanksgiving in *The Book of Common Prayer* speaks in some way about a future time when Jesus will come again.

• In Rite One, we give glory to God for the Sacrament, "a perpetual memory of (Christ's) precious death and sacrifice, until his coming again."

• In Rite Two, Prayer A (p. 363), we join in saying:
 Christ has died.
 Christ is risen.
 Christ will come again.

In that same prayer, we ask: "at the last day bring us with all your saints into the joy of your eternal kingdom."

• Prayer B includes the words, "We await his coming in glory" (p. 368). And we pray: "bring us to that heavenly country where, with all your saints, we may enter the everlasting heritage of your sons and daughters" (p. 369).

• See also Prayer C: "we await the day of his coming" (p. 371).

• In Prayer D, we celebrate Christ's death and ascension, "awaiting his coming in glory" (p. 374).

Jesus' Promise

Our belief in Jesus' coming again is rooted in promises found in the New Testament.

John's Gospel reports on a dialogue Jesus had with his disciples just after they left the Last Supper. He told them that he was going to a place where they could not join him.

Peter asked, "Lord, where are you going?"
Then Jesus shared these comforting words:

"Do not let your hearts be troubled. Believe in God, believe also in me. In my Father's house there are many dwelling places. If it were not so, would I have told you that I go to prepare a place for you? And if I go and prepare a place for you, *I will come again* and will take you to myself, so that where I am, there you may be also." (See *John 13:31-14:4*.)

No one knows when or how Jesus' coming again will take place. But it has been the faith of the Church from the beginning that the reign of God will be complete. Sin and death will no longer have any hold on humankind. The rule of Christ in people's hearts will bring joy forever.

This faith of Christians makes it possible for us to speak about the Holy Eucharist as a "foretaste" (a sampling) of the "heavenly banquet" when we shall all share in the glory of God's kingdom. Following the Great Thanksgiving, we always pray as Jesus taught us:

Our Father, who art in heaven,
> hallowed be thy Name,
> *thy kingdom come,*
> thy will be done,
>> on earth as it is in heaven.

PART IV
Outline of Faith

1. The Catechism

In the early years of the Church, a person who was preparing to be baptized was called a "catechumen" (meaning "one being taught"). For about three years a catechumen would receive instruction in the Christian faith.

By the time of the Middle Ages, this kind of teaching had largely disappeared. Most people were baptized as infants and grew up in the Church.

At the time of the Protestant Reformation, in the sixteenth century, there was a new desire to teach people more thoroughly about the beliefs of Christians. That is when the word "catechism" began to be used. It is the name for a printed series of short questions and answers that outline major beliefs.

In 1529, the German Reformer, Martin Luther, published a catechism that became widely known. Its questions were about the Creed, the Lord's Prayer, and the Ten Commandments. Within a few years, English "primers" (school readers for children) began to include short explanations of the faith. Then Archbishop Thomas Cranmer included a Catechism in the 1549 Prayer Book—with questions on baptism, the Apostles' Creed, the Trinity, the Ten Commandments, the duty of Christians toward God and their neighbors, and the Lord's Prayer.

Cranmer's catechism was intended to help young persons prepare for confirmation. A rubric (printed instruction) required that a priest use the questions for teaching in the church for one-half hour every six weeks, just before Sunday Evening Prayer.

Since then, all Prayer Books have contained a catechism. Revisions and additions have occurred through the generations. Questions on the sacraments have been added.

The present 1979 version of *The Book of Common Prayer*, which is used in the Episcopal Church in the United States, contains "An Outline of the Faith commonly called the Catechism" (pp. 845-862). It is longer than any previous catechism.

Following is a list of the main headings. An asterisk (*) appears after the titles that are not found in earlier Prayer Book catechisms:
Human Nature*
God the Father
The Old Covenant*
The Ten Commandments
Sin and Redemption*
God the Son
The New Covenant*
The Creeds
The Holy Spirit
The Holy Scriptures*
The Church
The Ministry
Prayer and Worship
The Sacraments
Holy Baptism
The Holy Eucharist
Other Sacramental Rites
The Christian Hope*

The Prayer Book explains, on page 844, that the Catechism is intended as an outline for teaching. It is also helpful for strangers who pick up a Prayer Book and wish to know what the Church teaches.

The different sections of the Catechism may be used in simple services of worship or in study groups. We do not need to feel that the questions and answers must be memorized and recited. Nor do they need to be examined one after another, in order.

The New Covenant

For believing Christians, a place to begin in the Catechism might be with the section, "The New Covenant" (pp. 850-851). This is one of the headings that was added for the 1979 Prayer Book.

A covenant is a special relationship involving a binding promise. God made such covenants with Noah, Abraham, and Moses. Each time, God had promised to be with their families and descendants. The covenant with Moses included the giving of the Law, the Ten Commandments. (See the Catechism heading, "The Old Covenant," pages 846-847.)

Through the long history of Israel and of Judah, the people failed to keep their promise of obedience to God. The prophet Jeremiah wrote about a time when God would offer a "new covenant"—not written on stone tablets but in the hearts of people. (See *Jeremiah 31:31*.)

When Jesus shared the cup at the Last Supper, he said, "This is the new covenant in my blood." (See *Luke 22:20*.) As he said this, the disciples would surely remember Jeremiah's words. Jesus, the long-awaited Messiah, was establishing a new relationship between God and humankind. Through faith in him we obtain forgiveness of sins and hope of everlasting life.

But the New Covenant was not a substitute or replacement for the Old. Rather, it is a fulfilling or completing of what God began among the chosen people of Hebrew history.

This Catechism section includes a question about the Summary of the Law: "You shall love the Lord your God with all your soul and with all your mind. This is the first and great commandment. And the second is like it: You shall love your neighbor as yourself." (See *Mark 12:28-31* and *Deuteronomy 6:4*.)

This is followed by a question on the New Commandment from Jesus: "Love one another." (See *John 13:34-35.*)

2. God in Three Persons

The Catechism contains three separate sections on God the Father, God the Son, and The Holy Spirit. Together, they describe what we believe about the Trinity.

The New Testament does not spell out how we understand One God in three Persons. An early hint of this "trinity" (threeness) can be found in the closing sentence of Paul's second letter to the church at Corinth:

"The grace of the Lord Jesus Christ, the love of God, and the communion of the Holy Spirit be with all of you" *(II Corinthians 13:13).*

Another hint is found at the end of Matthew's Gospel, as Jesus says to the eleven disciples:

"Go therefore and make disciples of all nations, baptizing them in the name of the Father and of the Son and of the Holy Spirit, and teaching them to obey everything that I have commanded you" *(Matthew 28:19-20).*

Here is a summary of what the Catechism teaches:

God the Father (p. 846). God made everything in heaven and earth. God's universe is good, and God loves and provides for all created things. We are to enjoy and care for every creature. Our way of knowing about God the Creator is through a community created by a covenant.

God the Son (pp. 849-850). Jesus is the perfect image of God the Father, and he shows us that God is love. We learn from the Creeds what he has done for us. We share in his victory over sin, suffering, and death when we are baptized into the New Covenant (as members of Christ's body, the Church).

The Church's first great Council (at Nicaea, in 325 CE), affirmed that Jesus Christ is "one being with the Father"—a fully equal person of the Trinity. This is a central belief of the Church.

God the Holy Spirit (pp. 852-853). The Spirit is "God at work in the world." In the Old Covenant, the Holy Spirit is the "giver of life" who spoke through the prophets. Christians know the presence of the Holy Spirit when they confess that Christ is Lord and "are brought into love and harmony with God, with ourselves, with our neighbors, and with all creation."

The Book of Common Prayer contains the following Collect (Of the Holy Trinity, p. 251):

> Almighty God, you have revealed to your Church your eternal Being of glorious majesty and perfect love as one God in Trinity of Persons: Give us grace to continue steadfast in the confession of this faith, and constant in our worship of you, Father, Son, and Holy Spirit, for you live and reign, one God, now and for ever. *Amen.*

3. The Church

The Catechism's questions about the Church are based on the Nicene Creed's description of it as "one, holy, catholic, and apostolic." These words were chosen with care to help us understand our life and work as the Church's members.

• *The Church is one.* When we look around us at the names of all the different churches in our communities, we may think to ourselves that the Church is badly divided. Christians do not agree on what they believe, on how they worship, or even on what they are supposed to do. Sometimes they quarrel and injure one another.

We realize our great need for the prayer, "For the Unity of the Church" *(The Book of Common Prayer* (p. 818):

> O God the Father of our Lord Jesus Christ, our only Savior, the Prince of Peace: Give us grace seriously to lay to heart the great dangers we are in by our unhappy divisions; take away all hatred and prejudice, and whatever else may hinder us from godly union and concord; that, as there is but one Body and one Spirit, one hope of our calling, one Lord, one Faith, one Baptism, one God and Father of us all, so we may be all of one heart and of one soul, united in one holy bond of truth and peace, of faith and charity, and may with one mind and one mouth glorify you; through Jesus Christ our Lord. *Amen.*

In this prayer we confess "the great dangers" of our "unhappy divisions," and we pray for unity among Christ's people. The word "one" is used twelve times. Included is all of *Ephesians 4:4-6,* which describes the Christian life.

To illustrate our oneness as Christians, the apostle Paul compared the Church's members to the parts of a human body. No part of the body can reject another part. When one part suffers, the whole body suffers. (See *I Corinthians 12:12-26*.) The oneness of Christians comes from the one Head of the Church who is Jesus Christ.

As a community of the New Covenant, we share a common life and have a "mission" (a job to do), sharing the good news of Christ and serving all the people of the world. We work for justice, peace, and love.

• ***The Church is holy.***

The word "holy" is related to "whole." The Holy Spirit is present in the Church, drawing us together and guiding us. The Spirit seeks to bring wholeness into all our relationships.

• ***The Church is catholic.***

The word "catholic" means universal—extending everywhere. All Christians are called by the same Lord, baptized into the worldwide body we call the Church, and inspired by the same Spirit.

In spite of the churches' many names and all the differences among us, we recognize that everyone who accepts Christ as Lord and Savior is a member of the catholic community. The one faith of Christians is being shared all around the earth all the time.

• ***The Church is apostolic.***

We can read in *Acts 2:43* about what happened after the Day of Pentecost: "Awe came upon everyone, because many wonders and signs were being done by the apostles."

Apostles are "the ones sent out." The work of the Twelve followed Peter's sermon, when thousands of new believers asked to be baptized. As the Church continued to grow, the apostles chose assistants. They "laid hands" on them, prayed for the presence of the Holy Spirit, and welcomed them as fellow laborers. (See *Acts, ch. 6*.)

Through the generations, century after century, God calls individuals and sends them out as the ordained leaders of the Church. They teach, preach, baptize, and serve others in Christ's name. All other baptized people also have a ministry to perform as we serve God and our neighbors, both in Christian congregations and in the larger community. Christian people are the spiritual descendants of the Twelve Apostles, and that is why we call the church "apostolic."

4. The Creeds

Persons being baptized in the early Church would be asked to stand before the congregation and say what they believed. Each one would declare, "I believe that Jesus Christ is the Son of God."

In time, short and simple statements like that one were expanded into what we now call the Apostles' Creed. In *The Book of Common Prayer,* this Creed is included in the Daily Office (Morning and Evening Prayer, pp. 53, 66, 96, and 120).

Each time we say the Apostles' Creed, we are reminded of our own baptisms. The Baptismal Covenant (BCP, p. 304) begins with three questions about belief in God as Father, Son, and Holy Spirit. The people's answers are from the Creed.

Beliefs Defined

Another reason for having a written creed is to make clear just what the Church teaches about the Christian faith. The major example is the Nicene Creed, which we say together at the Holy Eucharist just after the sermon.

This Creed is the work of the Council of Nicaea that met in 325 CE. (Nicaea was a city of ancient Bithynia, located in present-day Turkey.) This was the Church's first great Council, and it settled a big argument among Christian leaders.

How was the man Jesus related to God? Some persons doubted that he shared God's nature. A scholar named Athanasius persuaded the Council that Jesus Christ is "of one Being with the Father." From that time on, the Church took its stand that Jesus was both fully human and fully God. This mystery has been preserved in the words of the Nicene Creed.

Many scholars of Christian worship believe it is best for the congregation to say the Nicene Creed with the words, "We believe . . . ," rather than "I believe . . . ." We are confessing together as a congregation what the whole church believes, not just our personal convictions.

'Ancient Document'

The Catechism refers to an "ancient document" that is called the Athanasian Creed. It is found in *The Book of Common Prayer,* pages 864-865.

This statement was probably written in the fifth century in southern Gaul (France). Athanasius had nothing to do with it, but it is named for him because it reflects what he taught.

The Athanasian Creed is not used in public worship. It is included in our Prayer Book because it underlines our belief in the Trinity.

5. Sinners Redeemed

The Catechism includes a section titled "Sin and Redemption" (pp. 848-849). From it we learn that God has set us "free from the power of evil, sin, and death" through the work of Jesus Christ, who is the Messiah.

In the beginning, we were made "in the image of God" *(Genesis 1:26-27)*. As the Catechism puts it, "this means that we are free to make choices: to love, to create, to reason, and to live in harmony with creation and with God" (p. 845). It is God's will that we live in a close and loving relationship with our Creator.

But the sad fact is that we break our relationship with God. We do not live up to our part of the covenant. We do what *we* prefer more often than we do what God wants. To put it another way, we "rebel." All our relationships are spoiled by this condition that we call *sin*.

None of us is free from sin: "all we like sheep have gone astray" *(Isaiah 53:6)*.

So what can be done about our situation? What would set things right?

The good news of our faith is that Jesus Christ has come to "redeem" us—to make us whole again and to set us back into a right relationship with God. This great act on the part of a loving God was described by the Hebrew prophets as the work of the Messiah who would come.

Christians understand that Jesus of Nazareth was the long-expected Messiah. He redeemed us through his life, death, and resurrection. In turning our lives over to him as our Savior, we are set free from sin's power. If we are faithful in confessing the wrongs we have done, God is faithful to forgive.

Why Does Sinning Continue?

If we say that sin has been defeated, why does it continue? How do we explain all the wrongs and hurts that people bring upon one another?

Even though the victory over sin was won by Jesus long ago, it will not be recognized by everyone until the day of God's reign (kingdom).

Our situation is something like what happens in sports. At some point in a game, a team will begin to out-score its opponent. We say that they are winning, or have already won. But the game continues until the clock runs out and a bell sounds the end. Only then can we declare who won for sure.

As people of faith, we can already see that Jesus Christ has scored a win over sin and evil in the world. But the time has not yet come when his great work is known to all. Life continues as a struggle for us until the final coming of God's reign.

6. Prayer and Worship

How do we respond to someone who offers us gifts? We like to stay close to that person. And it is good to pass along the kindness we have received to other people.

This is how it can be when we think about all that God has given us. The greatest gift of all is Jesus Christ. We need to respond to God's goodness by coming near in our thoughts. And it is right for us to share the kindness of God by reaching out to others in helpful deeds.

Our life with God is called prayer. The Catechism says that our praying is "responding to God, by thought and by deeds, with or without words" (p. 856).

All through every day we can and do communicate with God. Our thoughts and deeds proceed spontaneously, mostly without a lot of planning and rehearsing.

Much of our worship is private. We pray alone in our own way.

It is also important that we meet with other Christians to pray together. We call this "corporate" worship—the prayers of the whole body of believers. (The word "corporate" comes from the Latin *corpus,* meaning "body.")

In both private and corporate worship, we may be grateful for forms to follow. The Daily Office and the Eucharist are the most common ways of praying formally. Many other liturgies are provided in the Prayer Book for special times and events in our lives.

Jesus recognized our need for patterns of praying when he taught us, "Our Father, who art in heaven. . . ." Within the great Collects and longer prayers of the Prayer Book, we can locate the seven kinds of praying that are outlined in the Catechism:

Adoration. To "adore" is to look upon another with deepest adoration and love. Our prayers of adoration are our effort to tell God how much we love being with the One who made us.

Praise. Prayers of praise declare the great worth of God. We celebrate God's holiness, power, and majesty —not in order to get something more for ourselves but simply because the very Being of God draws forth from us our deepest appreciation for God's greatness.

Thanksgiving. We give thanks to God for every blessing we enjoy, especially for families, friends, and neighbors. We give thanks for food, clothing, shelter, and work to do. And above all, we give thanks for our redemption and for everything that draws us nearer to God.

Penitence. We confess the wrongs we have done and all our sins. We ask to be forgiven, and we seek God's help in doing what is right.

Oblation. An oblation is an offering. We give ourselves to God along with our material gifts for God's work in the world. We ask that these offerings will be used for God's purposes.

Intercession. We ask God to help other people—the sick, the friendless, the poor, the sorrowing and the dying, and all others in need.

Petition. To present a petition is to ask something for ourselves. We bring our own needs to God. Although we may ask for many things, we are to follow the example of Jesus who prayed to God, "Your will be done."

7. Christian Ministry

All baptized people have a ministry of Christ to be carried out in the world.

The word "minister" stands for a person who serves as an agent or representative for another. In England, for example, the departments of government are held by Ministers who represent the Crown and the Parliament as they carry out their duties. They are like the Secretaries in our President's cabinet.

In a very real way, each Christian is someone who represents Christ and his church. We are all ministers.

The Catechism describes four kinds of ministers: lay persons, bishops, priests, and deacons. We commonly speak of them as "orders of ministry."

Bishops, priests, and deacons are members of Holy (Sacred) Orders. But all forms of Christian service, both ordained (clergy) or non-ordained (lay), are honored in the Church. We all have plenty of work to do for our Lord.

The New Testament does not offer clear descriptions of bishops, priests, and deacons.

The tradition of having priests in the Church comes from the practice of the Hebrews. We can read about priests in the Temples of Old Testament times. The Church's priests have similar duties. They serve as pastors (shepherds) of their congregations, assist their bishops as needed, preach the Gospel, administer the sacraments, and bless and pardon people in God's name.

The word for bishop is the Greek *episkopos,* which means "overseer." The Episcopal Church gets its name from that word. It is a church ruled by bishops. They carry out their ministries chiefly in dioceses (geographical regions).

The word deacon comes from the Greek *diakonos,* which means "attending servant." The early deacons served meals to the poor, visited the sick, and assisted priests with the sacraments.

The offices of bishop and deacon are similar to roles of people in the Greek culture of the early Church.

The Work of Lay Persons

Our 1979 Prayer Book recognizes lay persons as an order of ministry. They are mentioned first in the answer to the Catechism question, "Who are the ministers of the Church?"

The Greek word for people is *laos,* and that is where we get our word "laity" (lay persons). The apostle Paul and the writer of *I Peter 10:4-10* spoke of the ministry of all Christian believers. In 96 CE, St. Clement, one of the Church Fathers, wrote a letter that described lay persons as an order of ministers. Much later, the Protestant Reformation lifted up the idea of every Christian as an honored servant of God.

Children, young people—all can serve as Christ's ministers in the world. We do this by the way we live each day, at home, at school, at work, and in our recreation. Also, we serve by taking on jobs in the Church.

All of us, as members of the community of Jesus Christ, are being noticed by the people around us. Will they see in each of us the qualities of a Christian?

8. Christian Hope

The Catechism of our Prayer Book ends with a section titled "Christian Hope." It has to do with "last things"—what we believe about the end of life and the purpose of it all.

Most of us have heard of people who have "lost hope." They feel desperate, lonely, and miserable. Sometimes these feelings are caused by very real problems, such as a failing grade, a lost job, a broken friendship, family troubles, conflicts with others, or poverty and homelessness. (In Morning Prayer, we sometimes pray, "Let not the hope of the poor be taken away.")

At other times we feel hopeless for reasons we cannot quite understand.

The message of the Christian faith is that God has given us a final hope that cannot be destroyed, no matter what pain our daily lives may bring. Our final hope is in Christ and the completing of "God's purpose for the world."

Another important word for us is "assurance." We need to hear comforting words, to have someone reach out to us with news that gives us fresh courage.

The assurance of Christians is described in the final answer of the Catechism (p. 862). It is based on the apostle Paul's words in *Romans 8:38-39:*

> "For I am convinced that neither death, nor life, nor angels, nor rulers, nor things present, nor things to come, nor powers, nor height, nor depth, nor anything else in all creation, will be able to separate us from the love of God in Christ Jesus our Lord."

To put it very simply, we are so closely bound to our Lord that nothing at all can pull us away from him. What could be more reassuring than this good news?

Meanwhile, we still have questions about death and dying, and about the day of God's final judgment. Short, dependable answers are provided in the Catechism:

Christ's coming. This will be a time when our Lord's power will be known to all. He will make "all things new." (See *Revelation 21:5.*)

Heaven and hell. To share in heaven is to be forever with God. Such a presence is to be enjoyed. To exist in hell is to be separated from God forever.

Prayers for the dead. Persons who die are still within the circle of our love. We pray that they will grow in God's love.

Last judgment. Christ will come in glory and judge both the living and the dead.

Resurrection of the body. God raises us from death so that we are completely ourselves and can live with Christ along with all the saints.

Communion of saints. This is the whole family of God, both living and dead. It includes people we love and those "whom we hurt," and we are all held together in Christ "by sacrament, prayer, and praise."

Everlasting life. We enjoy a new way of being, united with all God's people, knowing God fully and loving God and one another.

Questions Continue

The Catechism is an "outline" for learning what we believe as Christians. Its questions suggest a brief summary of what the Church teaches—a "point to start from" as we explore our faith.

The answers that are given are not meant to shut off our sense of wonder. We live with the mysteries of God. All through our lives we think, study, and listen. New questions arise constantly, and it is good for us to ponder them.

In the community of faith, we share our doubts and anxieties with one another. In the end, we say to our Lord, "I believe. Help my unbelief." (See *Mark 9:24.*)

9. The Spirit Leads

Neither the Catechism nor anything else in the Prayer Book would be possible if it had not been for what happened at the first Pentecost.

It was the Jewish Feast of Weeks. (Pentecost means "fiftieth day," the Greek name for the celebration.) This was a period of thanksgiving seven weeks after the beginning of the barley harvest around the time of Passover. The Passover included a raising (waving) of the sheaf, based on the instructions in *Leviticus 23:9-14*.

By the time of Jesus, the festival of Pentecost also celebrated the giving of the Law to Moses on Mt. Sinai.

Following the resurrection, the disciples were uncertain about their future. What were they to do? They waited and prayed together in Jerusalem. In *Acts, ch. 2,* we can read about their amazing experience:

Many people had gathered in the city for the festival, from many nations. The disciples were all in the same house. Suddenly they heard a sound "like the rush of mighty wind" from heaven.

"Tongues of fire" rested over the disciples' heads. They began to speak in a way that made sense to the crowds who gathered around, even though they spoke different languages. Each person could understand!

The people wondered what it all meant. Were the disciples drunk with new wine? Peter stood and spoke in a loud voice. He assured everyone that no one was drunk. Instead, he said, this event was the outpouring of the Spirit of the Lord—just as the prophet Joel had predicted. (See *Joel 2:8-32*.)

Peter went on to preach with great power about Jesus of Nazareth. He had been crucified, but he had risen from the dead. He was the Messiah.

The crowd was deeply moved. They asked, "What should we do?"

Peter answered, "Repent, and be baptized every one of you in the name of Jesus Christ so that your sins may be forgiven; and you will receive the gift of the Holy Spirit" *(Acts 2:37)*.

About three thousand people were baptized. "They

devoted themselves to the apostles' teaching and fellowship, to the breaking of bread and the prayers" *(v. 42)*.

This was the beginning of the Church.

Prayers for Guidance

Through the centuries of the Church's history, Christians have faced many trials and challenges. At times many were persecuted and killed for their faith.

Sometimes power and wealth cause the Church's leaders to forget their real mission in the world. And sometimes Christians fall into sin and disobey God.

But the Holy Spirit does not leave the Church. We are offered guidance when we seek it in earnest prayer. When Christians disagree and divisions come, the Spirit's power can lead to peaceful solutions. Enemies can be brought together. Decisions can be reached. Beliefs can be defined more clearly.

In our time, the Church frequently faces a world that does not take religion seriously. Many very real problems face the people of God as they struggle to speak the good news of Jesus Christ to the modern world.

We are comforted and given strength as we remember the very words Peter quoted from the prophet Joel:

> 'In the last days it will be, God declares,
> that I will pour out my Spirit upon all flesh,
> and your sons and your daughters shall prophesy,
> and your young men shall see visions,
> and your old men shall dream dreams . . . .'
> —*Acts 2:17*